ABOUT THE AUTHOR

LeRoy Eims is director of evangelism worldwide for The Navigators, an international organization training laymen to reproduce their life-changing relationship with Christ in the lives of others. As a marine machine gunner, Eims watched a buddy die on a South Pacific beachhead, pleading for someone to tell him about God. Eims was unable to tell him but vowed to learn about God for himself.

Back home in Iowa, Eims married and went to work for the Chicago Great Western Railroad. He began to attend church and to search the Scriptures diligently. In time he settled the sin problem in his life as he trusted Christ as Saviour. He then dedicated himself to helping others find new life in Christ.

This book is an outgrowth of his sharing ministry and is chock-full of experiences in witnessing and practical witnessing methods.

Mr. Eims' Navigators work has taken him on three preaching tours in the Orient, two in Europe, and one in the Middle East.

He and his wife, Virginia, have three children, Larry and Becky, both in their 20s, and Randy, in his late teens.

DEDICATION

To Virginia, my beautiful, brown-eyed, blond partner, whose life has radiated a steady glow of inspiration and encouragement.

the adventure of sharing Christ

LeRoy Eims

While this book is designed for the reader's personal use and profit, it is also intended for group study. A leader's guide is available from your local bookstore or from the publisher at 95¢.

Published by
VICTOR BOOKS
a division of SP Publications, Inc.
WHEATON, ILLINOIS 60187

Library of Congress Catalog Card No. 74-77319
ISBN 0-88207-707-4

VICTOR BOOKS
A division of SP Publications, Inc.
P.O. Box 1825 ● Wheaton, Ill. 60187

CONTENTS

FOREWORD

Out of his years of experience as a staff member of The Navigators, LeRoy Eims writes with the smell of the smoke of the battle on his clothes. In *Winning Ways* he does not give us the theories of an arm-chair general, but the practical experiences of a man who has spent his life communicating the Gospel to individuals in groups. The ring of realism comes through in this book time after time.

Never before in our generation has there been such openness and spiritual hunger all over the world. Every Christian has the responsibility and privilege of being a witness to Jesus Christ, and this is a practical guide as to how it can be done. The author shows how to get started in conversation, how to explain the Gospel, how to answer some common objections, and how to follow-up a new Christian.

Confidence in the power of Scripture to convict or convert as the Holy Spirit uses it, and confidence in the power of prayer come through time after time.

There are many illustrations of spiritual truth which the reader will be able to use in his own conversation.

The number of realistic books on evangelism which combine spiritual principles with practical experience-tested instruction is very small. *Winning Ways* will take its place among them, and I commend it to all believers with confidence and enthusiasm.

PAUL E. LITTLE

International Congress on World Evangelization
Lausanne, Switzerland
March 1974

PREFACE

God has brought scores of men across my path who have profoundly affected my life. Space does permit a listing of them, but one must be singled out: Dawson Trotman, the founder of The Navigators.

Trotman visited Northwestern College in Minneapolis during my freshman year there and spoke in chapel. The following weekend a few of us went to a conference where he and his colleague Lorne Sanny were the main speakers. As these two men of God spoke, the Lord used them to set the course of my life.

A few months later Daws returned to the college for an evening rally. As he told us of the spiritual needs of the world, his eyes filled with tears and he began to sob. Several minutes passed before he regained his composure and continued to tell us of the world's hungry hearts. I left that meeting asking God to give me the same sort of burden for lost men.

This book shares some of the lessons God has patiently taught me in witnessing for Him the past 25 years. My prayer is that the Lord will use it to help you lead many people into the joy of knowing Him.

1

JESUS HAS
A PROBLEM

Jesus Christ has a problem, a big problem. Yes, He is the omnipotent Son of God, and He has loyal followers around the world, but our ascended Lord has faced one problem ever since His days on earth.

In Jesus' own words, the problem is stated in John 4:35—"Do you not say, 'Four months more and the harvest will be here?' Look, I tell you; raise your eyes and look at the fields, how they are white for harvest" (BERK).

Do you believe those words—that many people, more people than Christians dare to hope—are waiting to hear the Gospel of Christ and receive Him into their lives? Jesus wouldn't have said it if it weren't true, but most of His followers refuse to believe it. That's Jesus' problem.

If Jesus has a problem convincing Christians of the evangelistic opportunities around them, the devil also has a problem. He must keep Christians believing that most people do not want to hear about the way of salvation. And he must do this contrary to the teachings of Jesus in the Word of God, contrary to the repeated encouragements of

9

Gospel preachers, and contrary to the spiritual hunger manifesting itself today in every direction.

Apparently Satan is quite convincing, because the great majority of Christians are silent about God's Good News. In this book I want to expose Satan's lie and help Christians act on Jesus' truth. My experience over the past 25 years is that almost everyone is at least willing to listen to the story of God's love—and that many of the listeners are ready to invite the Saviour into their hearts.

A Man Named Israel

An encounter in Bellingham, Wash. illustrates the openness of people today. I was riding down the street with a friend, Lyle Irvin. We noticed a young man marching down the sidewalk carrying a sign painted with the words: "Peace, Love, Forgiveness." He was dressed in burlap, had long hair, and was barefooted. We pulled over to the curb, got out of the car, and went over to ask him who he was. He said he was the final prophet and that he had written to the pope, to Billy Graham, and to someone in India announcing his arrival. He said his name was Israel, and he was suffering for the sins of humanity and declaring peace, love, and forgiveness to the world.

At the mention of "Israel," the Lord brought a passage of Scripture to my mind, so I took out my pocket testament and asked if Israel would read Romans 10:1-4: "Brethren, my heart's desire and prayer to God for Israel is, that they might be saved. For I bear them record that they have a zeal of God, but not according to knowledge. For they being ignorant of God's righteousness, and going about to establish their own righteousness, have not submitted themselves unto the righteousness of

God. For Christ is the end of the law for righteousness to every one that believeth."

I pointed out to this "Israel" that God's desire for all of us was that we might be saved. He became quite interested, so I held his sign and gave him the New Testament, and Lyle and I had him look up a few more Scriptures, mostly from the Book of Romans. As we talked, we asked if he had a Bible. He said he did, so we suggested he read the Book of Romans and see if God would speak to him. He was a very sincere young man—but sincerely wrong in his direction.

About a week later I was in San Francisco and called Lyle on an item of business. He reminded me of our conversation with Israel and happily announced that our friend had gone to his room and read the New Testament for many hours. As a result, he had given his life to Christ and afterward accompanied Lyle and some friends to give his testimony to other people.

The message of Jesus Christ is powerful, and people today are generally receptive to finding out what that message really is.

Jesus wants you and me to see people as they really are. He wants us to see the crowds of "Samaritan men" coming out of our offices, our schools, our shops, our armed services, and our neighborhoods who are ready to listen to the Gospel. He wants us to lift up our eyes and look on the whole world. Multitudes throughout the world are ready to respond to the Gospel, as a field of fully-ripe corn that's ready to be reaped. The fields *are now* "white for harvest."

One thing that stands out in my memory from boyhood on a farm in Iowa is the great deal of work at harvest season. My mother was busy cooking for the threshers; my father, brothers, and many neighbors were busy in the fields and bringing crops to the crib, the barn, and the bins; and I was busy carrying water to the workers. Those were exciting, satisfying days.

And that's the way Jesus sees our world today, even as He saw His own. "When He saw the multitudes, He was moved with compassion on them, because they fainted, and were scattered abroad, as sheep having no shepherd. Then saith He unto His disciples, 'The harvest truly is plenteous, but the laborers are few; pray ye therefore the Lord of the harvest, that He will send forth laborers into His harvest'" (Matt. 9:36-38).

But the problem prevails: "The laborers are few." Are the church members few? No. Are conference attendees few? No. Are laborers few? *Yes!* People who go out into the "fields" and work—Christians who go out into the world and tell others about Jesus Christ—are scarce. Tragedy of tragedies—a crop is waiting with few hands to reap it!

Not every person we meet wants to hear the Gospel or will listen, that is true. But more people will listen than we would ever imagine, and my witnessing experiences around the world convince me that the Holy Spirit has been ripening a harvest that our vision fails to see.

An Angry-Looking Young Man

A few summers ago I was in Boulder, Colo. At that time Boulder was a stopping-off place for hundreds of "street people" in their summer migration from the East Coast to Big Sur and the beaches of California. One evening some of them were invited to a home for a meal of brown rice and tea and a time of Christian sharing.

Following the meal, I shared my testimony and a short witness for Christ. I noticed that one young man seated on the floor directly in front of me was listening quite intently. With his fringed leather jacket, long hair with Indian band around his forehead, big boots, and slanted sunglasses, he looked mean and angry to me, not unlike a person associated with Hell's Angels or some such gang.

I finished my witness and then invited anyone who would like to talk privately afterward to do so. I had no sooner finished when this menacing guy leaped to his feet and headed toward me. I thought sure he was going to hit me, so I quickly sat down, thinking: *People aren't supposed to hit anyone who's sitting down!*

I thought I had angered him with my talk about Jesus and sin and salvation, and was prepared for a violent reaction. To make matters worse, his bushy red-haired buddy came with him. But they sat down beside me on the floor, and the fellow with the sunglasses put his hand on my shoulder and asked in a very tender, quiet voice: "Do you know any reason why I can't come to Jesus?"

I was taken completely by surprise. I smiled, and said with a relieved sigh, "I can't think of a reason in the world, friend."

Then the double shocker: his red-haired buddy looked me in the eye and said, "Is this something that a Jew like me can get in on, or is it only for people like you?" I assured him there were no limits on this Good News. It was for everybody. He heaved a sigh of relief.

Later I asked myself: "Why did I expect a negative response? Am I prone to fear an unfavorable reaction when sharing the Gospel?"

This would be strange indeed because I can

count on the fingers of one hand the times when people have responded negatively or angrily to my witness. Certainly not all have received Christ, but much more often than not the conversation has been friendly, and the person has been genuinely interested and has left on a cordial note. But I suppose the distaste of possibly creating a scene or upsetting a person lurks near the back of my mind. Whatever it is, it has been an unwarranted fear.

God Will Fight for Us

The Scriptures tell us, "For God hath not given us the spirit of fear, but of power, and of love, and of a sound mind" (2 Tim. 1:7). Fear in witnessing is unwarranted because few will react negatively to a positive, kind witness, and because the Spirit of God in us will guide and protect us. I like to remember 2 Chronicles 32:8—"With him is an arm of flesh, but with us is the Lord our God to help us, and to fight our battles."

Bill Bright, founder of Campus Crusade for Christ, came to our home for three days in 1953. His objective was to help me get started in a campus witness. To begin, we went out on a hillside and prayed for the campus. What a thrill it was for me, a three-year-old Christian at that time, to pray with this man of God. Then we went to the campus and continued our prayer—this time praying as we walked its length and breadth. After saturating the place in prayer, Bill began to talk to students about Christ.

I watched with excitement as Bill chatted with one after another. And the most amazing thing happened! I had supposed the students in this sophisticated Eastern school would be either disinterested or somewhat belligerent. Wonder of wonders, they were wide open to talk about the Saviour! Some received Christ during those three days. It was a revelation to me to learn this simple truth—people will listen. The Lord used those days in my early Christian life to assure me of the present-day reality of the ancient scriptural truth: "Lift up your eyes, and look on the fields, for they are white already to harvest" (John 4:35).

The night before the Nixon-McGovern election in 1972, I was on a University of California campus. A young couple there had invited a few of their student friends to the house to discuss the Christian life. The group included long-hairs, short-hairs, straights, minority members, some adorned with beads, headbands, and fringed jackets, and some dressed in suits.

The one topic of the evening was Jesus and what it meant to live for Him. Driving home afterward, I asked the two guys with me if they had noticed anything strange about our evening. It hit me as being very peculiar that during three or four hours on a California campus the night before a hard-fought presidential election, no one had mentioned the election, President Nixon, or Senator McGovern. I realized then there is more interest in the things of Christ today than I have ever seen in my 25 years of being a Christian.

In Los Banos, a college town in the Philippine Islands located a few hours' drive from Manila, I was giving my testimony to an open meeting of students. A surprisingly large number had turned out to hear the presentation. After my message they had opportunity to comment or ask questions, using two microphones placed in the aisles halfway back on either side of the large auditorium.

Those students at the University of the Philippines at Los Banos are extremely intelligent. Many of them are hand-picked by governments of other lands to study agriculture at this school. It is one of the most prestigious schools in the Orient.

They began to ask their questions, and the clock ticked off one hour, then two, and was well into the third hour when I had to call the meeting to an end because of another appointment. I was sorry to close because there were still a half-dozen students lined up behind each microphone, patiently waiting and hoping to get their questions answered regarding the Person of Jesus Christ.

In Japan a recent fact-finding team of Asian Christian leaders interviewing college students gave this amazing report: 80% of the students did not have any serious religious affiliation. When asked which religious affiliation they would choose, if given a choice, 75% said they would choose Christianity. Fantastic!

My Navigator colleague Warren Myers found a widespread willingness to listen to the Gospel in Madras, India. At a training conference, the young men and women studied methods of witnessing, then paired off in teams of two and went into action. They went to a neighborhood of known Hindus, knocked on doors, and said: "Good afternoon, we are out talking to people about how Jesus Christ relates to life today. Could you spare a few minutes?"

In a little more than one hour, the 10 teams knocked on 22 doors and met 14 people who said, "Yes," they had time to talk. Of the 14, three made decisions for Christ. One of them had been witnessed to many times by a Christian.

Warren says: "I learned that most people will listen if you give them a choice, if the Gospel is clear, and if there is no pressure for a decision ✓ except from the Lord doing His inward work."

At the World Congress on Evangelism in Minneapolis in 1968, Warren led a workshop on witnessing. After the session, the members went out on the streets to practice what they'd learned. The teams prayed for the Lord's guidance in making contacts, then approached pedestrians with the greeting: "Good afternoon, we are out talking to people about how Jesus Christ relates to life today. Do you have a few minutes?"

They discovered that 50% of the people encountered were willing to stop and chat. This seemed like a very rewarding opportunity to the witnesses—more so than they had expected.

Warren accompanied a Presbyterian pastor one day and a Lutheran the next. Both had led many people to the Lord but never on the street in such a bold way. Each day the team approached six people, were granted the opportunity to talk about Christ with three, and saw one make a decision. In conversation afterward, the pastors agreed the decisions were made freely and clearly.

"Whether in America or overseas," Warren says, "people who are approached in a friendly way will give you an opportunity to present the Gospel even when rapport has not been established by prior friendship. I think rapport depends more on attitude than on length of association."

As a fairly new Christian, I worked in the mail-order shipping department of the Sears Roebuck store on Lake Street in Minneapolis. I was burdened to witness to the guys I worked with, and particularly one, "Big Swede." But for the life of me, I didn't know how to bring up the subject. I would try to screw up my courage, but day after day as we loaded trucks I kept putting it off. He was so big! What if he took offense and hauled off and slugged me? He could knock my head off, or at least loosen a few teeth. But the burden remained so I really began to pray about it. I promised the Lord the next time we had coffee break together I'd tell Big Swede about the power of the Gospel.

A few days after that prayer, the boss gave us a coffee break at the same time and I knew the moment had come. Not having the faintest idea what to say, I looked up at him and blurted: "Swede, are you born-again?"

He looked down and said, "No, but I've always wanted to be."

With 15 minutes left on the break, we went out back and stood under an old iron circular stairway. I presented Christ to him, and he was eager to pray. He closed his eyes and asked Christ into his heart!

That happened, not because I was a glib talker or had a clever approach or a polished witnessing technique. It happened simply because I spoke up and he was ready to respond—a prepared heart desirous of knowing God. I believe there are tens of thousands of people like that around the world, waiting for someone to give them the life-saving message.

Betty Cooper: Ready Witness

This kind of thing happens to other people, too. I read about Betty Cooper's ready witnessing in the *Power for Living* weekly paper.

Three sailors piled into the back seat of Mrs. Betty Cooper's 1962 Studebaker at the Alameda Naval Air Base hitchhiking station. All they wanted was a ride to Oakland, Calif., but they got more!

As soon as the doors slammed shut, Mrs. Cooper, a newspaper Linotype operator, asked each sailor his first name. Then, as her partner, Miss Jo Ferguson, drove, Mrs. Cooper took out a copy of her "Wordless Book" and some "Little Bibles" and began talking to the sailors about Jesus.

The sailors listened as attentively to the "Wordless Book" presentation as do the children in Mrs. Cooper's 14 Child Evangelism classes. After this, Mrs. Cooper said, "Jack, turn to page 28 and read it."

Jack read, " 'Christ died for our sins.' "

"Now read page 30," she told Tom.

" 'What must I do to be saved?' " Tom read that page's question.

"Read page 31," Mrs. Cooper said without looking at her booklet. She had all the pages memorized and followed a set approach like a salesman.

" 'Believe on the Lord Jesus Christ, and thou shalt be saved,' " Tom replied.

By this time they had arrived at their destination. Before they stopped, Mrs. Cooper asked the sailors if they wanted to receive the Saviour.

"Could you tell us more about Him?" Tom inquired.

Miss Ferguson parked the car near a public park. A half hour later all three sailors made professions of faith, took the "Little Bibles" and copies of *Power for Living*, and headed into the city.

Their second pickup at the hitchhiking station that night brought the two women some unusual passengers—two short, dark-complected merchant marine seamen. They had just returned from a trip to Saigon.

"I started to deal with them," Mrs. Cooper says,

"and they were wide-eyed to learn all about Jesus."

After they read the verses, she asked them, "What nationality are you?"

"We're from Yemen," one replied.

"Are you Arabs?" she asked.

"We're Jews. But we want to believe on Jesus," both assured her.

After a long discussion about the Saviour, one of the seamen asked, "Why doesn't someone go to Yemen to tell our people?"

"Maybe God wants you to tell them," she suggested.

On another trip, Mrs. Cooper recognized one of her back-seat riders. "Didn't I pick you up last week?" she asked.

"You sure did," sailor Dick answered. "I was furious when I went back to the base. I thought, *The nerve of that woman to say I wasn't saved.* But after I settled down, I told myself, *Dick, you're not saved.* I got down on my knees and asked Jesus to save me. And it has sure made a difference in my life!"

"Like a swift arrow hitting a bull's-eye," Mrs. Cooper told him. "The Word of God really penetrated your heart. I knew it would."

In his book *Say It With Love* (Victor Books), Dr. Howard Hendricks says, "I am convinced the world is more eager to hear our message than we are to deliver it. Never in my ministry have I seen such responsiveness and receptivity to the Gospel as in recent days."

In view of these exciting opportunities, do you choose to be a part of Jesus' "problem," or part of the solution?

2

JUST PLAIN
BILL AND BETTY

"Witnessing? *Me?* That's what we pay the preacher for! He's trained for it, and he has been called by God to preach the Gospel. I'm only an inexperienced Christian, with no gift of gab. Sorry, I'm just not cut out to be a witness."

Have you ever said or heard anything like that? I have. Most Christians think witnessing should be done by the professionally trained or especially gifted Christians. I've got news for you.

As a new Christian I heard a scholarly professor from Dallas Theological Seminary speak on Ephesians 4:11-12. The passage reads: "And He [*Christ*] gave some, apostles; and some, prophets; and some, evangelists; and some, pastors and teachers; for the perfecting of the saints, for the work of the ministry, for the edifying of the body of Christ."

The speaker pointed out the thrust of the verse: God has given divinely appointed men to train the people of God, so that ordinary, garden-variety Christians like you and me might go forth and accomplish His ministry in the family of faith and in the world. The pastors and teachers are commissioned to train the rest of us to do our spiritual work better. The Bible calls it "the perfecting of the saints."

It is interesting to note that the word "perfecting" in that verse is the same word used when the fishermen were "mending" their nets in Matthew 4:21! This makes quite a picture: we Christians show up at church and the preacher and other "ministers" mend us for our people-netting ventures wherever we go during the week!

Picture this. A U.S. Marine company in battle gear lands on a beach. The company saunters over to some palm trees and sits down on the ground to make daisy chains. All except the officer in command; he charges into the jungle, armed with an M1 slung over one shoulder, a Thompson submachine gun under one arm, grenades bristling from his belt, a .45 strapped on his boot, and a knife gleaming in his teeth.

A week later the warrior returns to the palm trees and the entire company greets him warmly. "It's great to see you! Keep up the good work!" They pat him—gingerly—on the back, patch up his wounds, replenish his ammunition, and urge him back into battle.

Ridiculous? Yes. Battles aren't fought and won that way. But quite often I see a similar scene in our churches. One man, the preacher, makes herculean efforts to win the spiritual battles, to take territory from Satan, while Christians on the sidelines hope and pray their leader will do better!

Is it possible that military men have more sense— or dedication—than a people who have the Book of God and are enlightened by the Spirit of truth? Possibly one answer is that most Christians don't recognize we're involved in *war*. True, we don't battle against flesh and blood, but, whether we realize it or not, we do struggle "against principalities, against powers, against the rulers of the darkness of this world, against spiritual wickedness in high places" (Eph. 6:12).

Since that is the case, Paul says, "Take unto you [*you ordinary Christians*] the whole armor of God, that ye may be able to withstand in the evil day, and having done all, to stand. Stand therefore, having your loins girt about with truth, and having on the breastplate of righteousness; and your feet shod with the preparation of the Gospel of peace; above all, taking the shield of faith, wherewith ye shall be able to quench all the fiery darts of the wicked. And take the helmet of salvation, and the sword of the Spirit, which is the Word of God: praying always with all prayer and supplication in the Spirit, and watching thereunto with all perseverance and supplication for all saints" (Eph. 6:13-18).

As Christians, we are the enemy and target of Satan. And we are members of Christ's army—though our Commander allows us to volunteer for duty or to battle our consciences instead.

God does appoint leaders to train and direct the troops, but God has always relied heavily on men in the ranks—those who rub shoulders with the masses.

Hebrews 11 tells us of heroes of faith through the ages, and look who they are: herdsmen, farmers, a boat builder, government administrators, military men. In the list there is only one religious leader mentioned—Samuel, the priest of God.

What does God tell us by this? He confirms that His work in the world has always been carried on by individuals who live among the people, knowing them, loving them, and speaking for God to them.

Ezekiel 22:30 speaks of the tragedy when God couldn't find such a person: "And I sought for a man *among them*, that should make up the hedge, and stand in the gap before Me for the land, that I should not destroy it: but I found none."

It's no mystery why God searches for a witness from among the people. Consider this scene: Several guys are standing around in a garage. Two men are working under a car, and one of them is a Christian. A preacher from a nearby church drops in to visit the Christian mechanic.

One of the bystanders announces: "Hey, Pete! The preacher is here to see you." The atmosphere crackles. It gets quiet and the conversation changes —temporarily. After the preacher leaves, the guys return to their normal language and actions.

Who could influence that garage the most for God: Pete, with grease under his fingernails and in his hair, working steadily and honoring his Master; or the preacher, making a brief contact with little real communication?

God is endlessly searching for a person *among them*. The Christian mechanic spends the same amount of time as his friends trying to wash off grease. He has the same trouble they do emptying an oil pan without making a big mess. He cuts his hands the same way they do. But he faces the same daily life *with Jesus*. Cannot he show the differences that Jesus makes much more clearly than the preacher? He can, if Pete loves the Lord and follows Him as we expect the preacher to do!

An Angel Can't Do It

The Apostle Paul says, "We were allowed of God

to be put in trust with the Gospel" (1 Thes. 2:4). That's a valuable trust! The Gospel is God's only way to save the eternal souls of lost men and women, boys and girls. It is His appointed message to transform the dreary, defeated lives of His creatures. And He has committed that Gospel to *us!*

If you were a military commander and had one bridge that maintained access to your objective, you would do all in your power to retain control of that bridge. The Christian's objective is to win men to Christ; God is the commander; and the Gospel is the bridge which stretches across life's chasm.

The Scriptures show that God's people alone have the privilege of sharing the Gospel of Christ. One confirmation of that fact is vividly revealed in Acts 10:1-6.

"There was a certain man in Caesarea called Cornelius, a centurion of the band called the Italian band, a devout man, and one that feared God with all his house, which gave much alms to the people, and prayed to God alway. He saw in a vision evidently about the ninth hour of the day an angel of God coming in to him, and saying unto him, 'Cornelius.' And when he looked on him, he was afraid, and said, 'What is it, Lord?' And he said unto him, 'Thy prayers and thine alms are come up for a memorial before God. And now send men to Joppa, and call for one Simon, whose surname is Peter; he lodgeth with one Simon, a tanner, whose house is by the seaside; he shall tell thee what thou oughtest to do.' "

Cornelius was an honest searcher for God. He was a bit shook when an angel came and spoke to him, and who wouldn't be! Notice that the angel gave him explicit instructions to send messengers to Joppa and ask for Peter, a man living with Simon, whose house was by the seaside. The meticulous angel left out an important matter: how to know and receive Jesus Christ, the Saviour. That Good News was destined to be communicated by ordinary mortals!

If he had chosen to do so, God could have written John 3:16 across the sky every day. Or He could have spelled it out in the stars. Instead, He has assigned the momentous mission of communicating the Gospel to us! What a privilege— and responsibility. Can you think of anything more important or exciting? Outside of our worship of God and walk with Him, this opportunity to share His life with others is the most satisfying experience I know.

Some years ago on a trip to the East Coast I visited a friend, King Coffman, who was an instructor at West Point Military Academy. We first met at a Christian conference in California when I was a college student and he was a cadet at the academy. In subsequent years he became an active witness for Christ in the Army.

While I was at King's home, some cadets came over for fellowship. They discussed the need to get a strong witness going in another barracks, the need for someone to prepare to lead a Bible study in a certain area, and other opportunities. So, Captain King Coffman was working with students at the academy who were becoming men of God and influencing still others for Christ. He was serving as God's man among men.

After leaving West Point, I stopped at an Air Force base and fellowshiped with one of the new chaplains. "Our biggest need," he said as he contemplated his new job, "is to have some good witnesses out in those barracks. We are lacking in vital witness among the men—in fact, it's even difficult to get a man to read the Scriptures on Layman Sunday!"

As I visited the barracks and places where the airmen spent their free time, I knew what that base needed. It needed another King Coffman—*a man among them*—but at that time God found none there.

Dispersion Conversions

Have you noticed how the laymen's ministry reached out in New Testament days? It is thrilling to behold. Acts 8 describes the fierce opposition against the Christians and their witness. "Saul was consenting unto his [*Stephen's*] death. And at that time there was a great persecution against the Church which was at Jerusalem; and they were all scattered abroad throughout the regions of Judea and Samaria, except the apostles. And devout men carried Stephen to his burial, and made great lamentation over him. As for Saul, he made havoc of the Church, entering into every house, and hailing men and women committed them to prison. Therefore they that were scattered abroad went everywhere preaching the Word" (vv. 1-4).

When persecution hit the Church, the Christian laymen thought it best to flee for their lives. The apostles remained in Jerusalem, possibly due to the protection encouraged by Gamaliel: "And now I say unto you, refrain from these men, and let them alone, for if this counsel or this work be of men, it will come to nought, but if it be of God, ye cannot overthrow it; lest haply ye be found even to fight against God" (Acts 5:38).

In Acts 11:19-21 we pick up the story of the

fugitive laymen. "Now they which were scattered abroad upon the persecution that arose about Stephen traveled as far as Phenice, Cyprus, and Antioch, preaching the Word to none but unto the Jews only. And some of them were men of Cyprus and Cyrene, which, when they were come to Antioch, spake unto the Grecians, preaching the Lord Jesus. And the hand of the Lord was with them, and a great number believed, and turned unto the Lord."

Notice that they went about "preaching the Lord Jesus," and God signally blessed their labors! "A great number believed and turned unto the Lord." The apostles had trained these laymen well. They found it natural to share Christ because they had been living in an atmosphere of dynamic witness. We see in Acts 2:23-24; 3:14-15; 4:10; and 5:30-31 that the death, burial, and resurrection of Christ was unflinchingly preached by the apostles.

Amid severe persecution the apostles unswervingly proclaimed Christ. "And to him [Gamaliel] they agreed; and when they had called the apostles, and beaten them, they commanded that they should not speak in the name of Jesus, and let them go. And they departed from the presence of the council, rejoicing that they were counted worthy to suffer shame for His name. And daily in the Temple, and in every house, they ceased not to teach and preach Jesus Christ" (Acts 5:40-42).

When the early Christian laymen went out on their own, they reflected the spirit of the environment in which they had been trained. God made these Christians "men among them" in Antioch, for "the disciples were called Christians first in Antioch" (Acts 11:26). Possibly it was a name to mock the followers of Christ, but they or we could not choose a nobler name. Christians—men and women who lived all-out for Jesus Christ.

Philip was one of the laymen who escaped Jerusalem during the purge. But he didn't go into hiding. "Philip went down to the city of Samaria and preached Christ unto them. And there was great joy in that city" (Acts 8:5, 8). Some time later Philip was led to a wilderness area where he met a traveler of high authority from Ethiopia. In response to the black man's question about the Scriptures, Philip "began at the same Scripture, and preached unto him Jesus" (Acts 8:35).

Philip, you recall, was not an apostle. He was one of the men chosen to serve tables, as recorded in Acts 6:5. But God had a faithful witness in this man—whether in city centers or desert wilderness. No one could have convinced this young layman that the fields were not "white for harvest."

Bill Bright, Campus Crusade for Christ director, tells of an incident that happened to him some years ago in Oklahoma. He was coming out of his hotel and saw a man on the sidewalk with a handful of Gospel tracts and some signs around him that read, "Jesus Saves"/"Repent Now"/"Ye Must Be Born Again." Bill glanced up the street and saw a well-dressed young couple coming toward this man, and realized that the man was preparing to "buttonhole" them and present them with "the fiery Gospel."

Instantly concerned that such an approach might offend the couple, Bill quickly turned back toward his room to get a copy of the neatly printed, logically presented Gospel pamphlet, "The Four Spiritual Laws." He hoped to engage the couple in conversation before the "fanatic" in the signboards confronted them.

As Bill emerged from the hotel, his heart sank.

The couple was already in conversation with the Gospel peddler. As Bill approached them, he heard the woman say she had become interested in the things of God and she was thankful for the tracts he had given her.

When Bill told this story to us, he looked at the dozen or so men present and said, "Gentlemen, God is so determined to get this message out that if we fail Him He will raise up stones to cry out the message of salvation."

But, of course, Bright spoke figuratively. The stones will not cry out.

No angel is going to share Christ with lost men and women, either. God is not going to write the message in the sky. Ministers can't get the job done by themselves. Jesus said to His worshipful followers: "Go ye into all the world, and preach [*proclaim*] the Gospel to every creature" (Mark 16:15).

And remember Paul's travel-tested confidence as you go: "I can do all things through Christ which strengtheneth me" (Phil. 4:13).

3

TELLING IT
LIKE IT IS

The courtroom is packed. The day is hot and muggy, and tempers are getting short. Tension in the air is thick. The defendant is nervous, on edge. Lawyers have been at each other all day employing every trick in the book. The prosecution calls another witness to the stand. After being sworn in he is asked where he was the night of April 7.

"Council Bluffs, Iowa," he replies.

The judge explodes. "Why was this person called?" he demands. "The crime was committed in Ocean City, Maryland!"

The chagrined witness leaves the stand amidst courtroom laughter and to the embarrassment of the prosecution.

Another witness takes the stand. He is also asked, "Where were you the night of April 7?"

The man's face grows sullen; he glares at the jury and mumbles: "I refuse to answer on the grounds that it might incriminate me."

After several attempts to get some response proves futile, the witness is dismissed.

A third man takes the stand. He, too, is asked,

"Where were you the night of April 7?"

"I was in Ocean City, Maryland, sir. I saw it all, and I can tell you everything you need to know."

Laughter again rings out and someone in the gallery shouts, "You tell 'em, buddy." This witness is known as the town liar.

The testimonies of these three men indicate some of the characteristics of witnesses. Let's look closer.

You Have to Know Something

First, a witness must know something about the subject. The early disciples of Christ were absolutely certain about their testimony: "That which we have seen and heard declare we unto you, that ye also may have fellowship with us; and truly our fellowship is with the Father, and with His Son Jesus Christ" (1 John 1:3).

Paul, who heard the risen Christ speak to him from the great light, was told: "The God of our fathers hath chosen thee, that thou shouldest know His will, and see that Just One, and shouldest hear the voice of His mouth. For thou shalt be His witness unto all men of what thou hast seen and heard" (Acts 22:14-15).

Our encounter with Christ is spiritual rather than physical and visible, but it is life-changing if genuine.

Before I met Christ, for example, I was hampered from doing what I was capable of because of weaknesses and faults which I came to recognize as deliberate sin and rebellion against God. Now I am free from that moral handicap and able to do good and avoid evil. I can tell others what's different since I met Christ and gradually learned to follow Him more closely.

Think through your own testimony and jot down pertinent facts as to what your life was like before you met Christ. This will help you speak convincingly of the fulfillment and joy Christ gives.

Before coming to know Christ, some people never feel quite right. No matter how well things go, they sense that something is "missing." Maybe they frequently sleep fitfully. This experience fits the biblical description: "'There is no peace,' saith the Lord, 'unto the wicked'" (Isa. 48:22).

This person faces the fact of sin in his life and receives Christ; then he begins to tell God the things that disturb him. Over a period of time, the unrest vanishes and Philippians 4:6-7 begins to blossom in his life: "The peace of God, which passeth all understanding" keeps his heart and mind through Christ Jesus.

Often a newborn Christian says, "When I asked Christ into my life, I felt like a ton of bricks slid off my shoulders." He has experienced Jesus' promise: "Come unto Me, all ye that labor and are heavy laden, and I will give you rest" (Matt. 11: 28). Maybe he didn't have the slightest notion he was carrying a burden until he asked Jesus into his life and received a lighter-than-air conscience.

Both of these examples demonstrate a witness for Christ, a testimony of what He has done specifically in a person's life. It is extremely important to be specific, like the blind man in John 9. He knew that he had been given his sight.

If you cannot think of some specific change since trusting Christ, ask God to show you one that will be helpful to cite to others. Or go to a Christian who has a clear testimony of Christ changing his life and ask him to help you focus on a strategic change. Like newborn babies, many of us need time to truly perceive the things we "see."

You also need to know clearly what happened that caused the change. You responded to the Gospel of Christ and asked Him into your life, and it is essential that listeners understand this. We aren't changed by following a moral code or doing good works; we are changed by Jesus Christ's entrance into our lives. The new life issues from a new birth, Jesus tells us (John 3:3). To share this experience in a way that will help others find the way, we must know the concepts and realities of the Gospel.

What are the basic truths of the Gospel?

Here is a quick biblical summary:

- Everyone has sinned against God (Rom. 3:12, 23).
- Because of sin, we all die (Rom. 6:23; 5:12).
- Death brings sinners to judgment before God (Heb. 9:27).
- Jesus died to take away mankind's sin (Rom. 5:8; 1 Peter 3:18).
- We must invite Jesus in to get sin out (Rev. 3:20; Rom. 10:9-10).
- When we believe in and receive Jesus, we have eternal life (1 John 5:11-12; John 3:16).

A good testimony for Christ contains three perspectives: *what your life was like before you knew Christ; what you did to be spiritually reborn; what your life with Christ is like now.*

Beyond the simple Gospel truths are treasures of knowledge that can illuminate the mysteries and quandaries of life. Paul used this knowledge to witness, as recounted in Acts 17:2. "And Paul, as his manner was, went in unto them, and three Sabbath Days reasoned with them out of the Scriptures." This kind of witness shows up throughout the ministry of the apostles.

On the Day of Pentecost the Apostle Paul said, "But this is that which was spoken by the Prophet Joel" (Acts 2:16), and he went on to quote Joel 2:28-32. Of course, that incident could have turned out another way. As Peter heard his co-laborers accused of being drunk, he might have protested: " 'This is that which was spoken by the Prophet Joel; and' . . . ah . . . er, Son, run to the Temple for me and bring the Joel scroll!"

Frankly, I doubt that would have worked well. Peter *knew* Joel 2:28-32, and he was empowered by his Teacher, the Holy Spirit. He hadn't prepared this as a "sermon"—he was out in the street surrounded by people, and when this incident occurred the Holy Spirit brought the Scriptures to mind which answered the questions of the skeptics.

Where did the apostles get this approach? Perhaps from the Master of earthly teachers, who repeatedly said: "It is written . . ." (Matt. 4:4, 7, 10). For three years the disciples lived with One who quoted the Old Testament Scriptures to enlighten and strengthen His hearers. Often He would ask people: "Have ye not read . . . ?" At one point He told them, "Do ye not therefore err, because ye know not the Scriptures, neither the power of God?" (Mark 12:24)

Jesus would tell us the same thing today. There is a general lack of knowledge of the Scriptures among the people of God.

I was having dinner with some students in one of our Christian schools. A student whose father was a pastor was talking to me about the Bible. I asked her, "Do you believe the Bible is the holy, inspired Word of God?"

"Yes, I surely do."

"Why do you believe that?" I asked.

"Why, that's what the church believes."

"Every member of the church?" I questioned.

"Well, no, I guess not every member."

"Why do you believe it?" I inquired again. "Let me ask you, do you know any passage of Scripture on the subject of the inspiration of the Bible?"

The student thought and said she was sure there was one somewhere, but she didn't know exactly where. That is a serious problem among Christians. On any biblical subject, that's too often the way it goes.

A statement by the risen Christ gives us an important guideline for our witnessing. "Ye shall receive power . . . and ye shall be witnesses unto Me" (Acts 1:8). Jesus' followers are to witness not to a plan but to a *Person*—the Person of Jesus Christ. It is easy to fall into a rut and to witness according to our prejudices or a pat plan. Our mission is to present Christ, nothing else. Note the Apostle Paul's statement in this regard in 1 Corinthians 2:1-2: "And I, brethren, when I came to you, came not with excellency of speech, or of wisdom, declaring unto you the testimony of God. For I determined not to know anything among you, save Jesus Christ, and Him crucified."

If I am to tell someone about Christ, the better I know Him the more I can tell. The biblical passages that follow reveal much about the Person and ministry of Jesus Christ. See how much you learn just from this reading.

The Word, Source of Life, and Eternal God

"In the beginning was the Word, and the Word was with God, and the Word was God. The same was in the beginning with God. All things were made by Him; and without Him was not anything made that was made. In Him was life; and the life was the light of men. And the light shineth in darkness; and the darkness comprehended it not" (John 1: 1-5).

"And the Word was made flesh, and dwelt among us (and we beheld His glory, the glory as of the only begotten of the Father), full of grace and truth" (John 1:14).

"For God so loved the world, that He gave His only begotten Son, that whosoever believeth in Him should not perish, but have everlasting life" (John 3:16).

"Father, I will that they also, whom Thou hast given Me, be with Me where I am, that they may behold My glory, which Thou hast given Me; for Thou lovedst Me before the foundation of the world" (John 17:24).

"And now, O Father, glorify Thou Me with Thine own self with the glory which I had with Thee before the world was" (John 17:5).

"I am come that they might have life, and that they might have it more abundantly" (John 10: 10b).

"Jesus saith unto him, 'I am the way, the truth, and the life; no man cometh unto the Father, but by me'" (John 14:6).

"Behold, a virgin shall be with Child, and shall bring forth a Son, and they shall call His name Emmanuel, which being interpreted is, 'God with us'" (Matt. 1:23).

"In Him [Christ] dwelleth all the fullness of the Godhead bodily" (Col. 2:9).

God a Man and Died for All Men

"Let this mind be in you, which was also in Christ

Jesus; who, being in the form of God, thought it not robbery to be equal with God; but made Himself of no reputation, and took upon Him the form of a servant, and was made in the likeness of men. And being found in fashion as a man, He humbled Himself, and became obedient unto death, even the death of the cross.

"Wherefore God also hath highly exalted Him, and given Him a name which is above every name; that at the name of Jesus every knee should bow, of things in heaven and things in earth, and things under the earth; and that every tongue should confess that Jesus Christ is Lord, to the glory of God the Father" (Phil. 2:5-11).

"For I came down from heaven, not to do Mine own will, but the will of Him that sent Me" (John 6:38).

"Therefore doth My Father love Me, because I lay down My life, that I might take it again. No man taketh it from Me, but I lay it down of Myself. I have power to lay it down, and I have power to take it again. This commandment have I received of My Father" (John 10:17-18).

"For I [Paul] delivered unto you first of all that which I also received, how that Christ died for our sins according to the Scriptures, and that He was buried, and that He rose again the third day according to the Scriptures" (1 Cor. 15:3-4).

"To Him give all the prophets witness, that through His name whosoever believeth in Him shall receive remission of sins" (Acts 10:43).

"Who hath delivered us from the power of darkness, and hath translated us into the kingdom of His dear Son; in whom we have redemption through His blood, even the forgiveness of sins; who is the image of the invisible God, the firstborn of every creature: for by Him were all things created, that are in heaven, and that are in earth, visible and invisible, whether they be thrones, or dominions, or principalities, or powers; all things were created by Him, and for Him, ind He is before all things, and by Him all things consist. And He is the head of the body, the Church; who is the beginning, the firstborn from the dead, that in all things He might have the preeminence. For it pleased the Father that in Him should all fullness dwell" (Col. 1:13-19).

Jesus Is Lord of Heaven and Earth

"And why call ye Me, 'Lord, Lord,' and do not the things which I say?" (Luke 6:46)

"Ye call Me Master and Lord; and ye say well; for so I am" (John 13:13).

"God, who at sundry times and in divers manners spake in time past unto the fathers by the prophets, hath in these last days spoken unto us by His Son, whom He hath appointed heir of all things, by whom also He made the worlds; who being the brightness of His glory, and the express image of His person, and upholding all things by the word of His power, when He had by Himself purged our sins, sat down on the right hand of the Majesty on high" (Heb. 1:1-3).

"Wherefore He is able also to save them to the uttermost that come unto God by Him, seeing He ever liveth to make intercession for them" (Heb. 7:25).

"And while they looked stedfastly toward heaven as He went up, behold, two men stood by them in white apparel; which also said, 'Ye men of Galilee, why stand ye gazing up into heaven? This same Jesus, which is taken up from you into heaven, shall so come in like manner as ye have seen Him go into heaven'" (Acts 1:10-11).

"For the Lord Himself shall descend from heaven with a shout, with the voice of the archangel, and with the trump of God; and the dead in Christ shall rise first; then we which are alive and remain shall be caught up together with them in the clouds, to meet the Lord in the air; and so shall we ever be with the Lord" (1 Thes. 4:16-17).

Perhaps we may hear Jesus say at this point: "If ye know these things, happy are ye if ye tell them" (see John 13:17). But you have to know them first.

You Have to Tell Something

The second quality of a good witness is that he is willing to talk. Like Philip, we must open our mouths and tell what we know about Jesus. This is a problem even for many Christians who have something vital to tell. There are many reasons for the failure.

One is *lack of boldness.* Now, boldness is not brashness—grabbing a guy by the collar or stopping him short with a, "Brother, are ya saved?" Boldness is simply courageous action in the face of opposition.

The Scriptures have quite a bit to say on boldness and how to get it into our lives. Let's look at six helps.

1. *Confess sin.* Proverbs 28:1 informs us: "The wicked flee when no man pursueth; but the righteous are bold as a lion."

God has spoken to my own heart through this verse. It is tough to talk to people about a wonderful Christian life if I am burdened by unconfessed sin on my soul. So one of the paths to a bold presentation of my Saviour is a generous application of 1 John 1:9: "If we confess our sins, He is faithful and just to forgive us our sins, and to cleanse us from all unrighteousness."

2. *Spend time communing with Jesus.* Acts 4: 12-13 tells us how Peter and John became knowledgeable witnesses. " 'Neither is there salvation in any other; for there is none other name under heaven given among men, whereby we must be saved.' Now when they saw the boldness of Peter and John, and perceived that they were unlearned and ignorant men, they marvelled; and took knowledge of them, that they had been with Jesus."

Spending time with Jesus is a good practice under any circumstance and for any reason. Close fellowship with the Lord Jesus Christ in daily prayer and reading His Word results in an overflow of His life to others. This is the abundant life: Jesus' joy and blessing filling us and spilling over to those around us.

3. *Pray for boldness.* The apostles prayed specifically for boldness to share Christ with others. "And now, Lord, behold their threatenings, and grant unto Thy servants, that with all boldness they may speak Thy Word" (Acts 4:29).

Do you ever find yourself in the situation the apostles were experiencing here? Have you felt the lack of boldness that sometimes results when you feel threatened? Have you prayed about it and asked the Lord for boldness to share the Word of Christ? You can, and God will answer that prayer —which is surely according to His will.

4. *Find a good example.* "And many of the brethren in the Lord, waxing confident by my bonds, are much more bold to speak the Word without fear" (Phil. 1:14).

This passage contains a great truth that has benefitted me personally. As a new Christian in Minneapolis, I met a man named Joe Noble. Joe volunteered to help me from time to time in my new walk with the Lord.

One day I had to go to Fort Snelling to check with the Veteran's Administration about the G. I. bill. Joe rode the bus out with me. On the way back I thought we should hitchhike and save the bus fare. Joe was agreeable to the idea and suggested we try for 10 minutes. If no car stopped we would take it from the Lord we were to ride the bus. That sounded good to me, so we stuck out our thumbs. After a few minutes a car stopped and we got in.

Joe sat in the front seat and talked, and I listened in amazement at what happened. Quietly, politely, and effectively, Joe engaged the driver in a conversation about spiritual matters. The driver was soon deeply involved, keenly interested. It was the first time I had ever "seen" an actual witnessing situation. I was thrilled. As a result I spent time with Joe whenever I had the opportunity. Just as the life and witness of the apostles gave others confidence to speak the Word, so Joe's life affected me.

If you know someone who is experiencing the joy of bringing others to Christ, spend as much time with that person as you can. God will teach you much as you see his life used of the Lord. This living "picture" is worth 10,000 words.

5. *Memorize Scripture.* The practice of Scripture memorizing affects our lives in many ways. Jeremiah 20:9 brings out one of them. "Then I said, 'I will not make mention of Him, nor speak anymore of His name.' But His Word was in mine heart as

a burning fire shut up in my bones, and I was weary with forbearing, and I could not stay."

As I fill my heart with God's Word, it becomes like a fire burning in my soul. I feel a compelling urgency to share Christ. We may get discouraged. People don't seem to be listening to our attempts to witness, so why speak? But if the Word of God is burning like a fire in our hearts, we are soon compelled once again to open our mouths and share the warmth.

6. *Don't wait for the perfect opportunity.* Ecclesiastes 11:4 warns us against this: "He that observeth the wind shall not sow; and he that regardeth the clouds shall not reap."

The devil is very clever and would like to convince us that the time is not right. "Put it off," urges a voice; "later will be a better time." However, if we wait for a perfect set of circumstances, we will wait a long time. I know of whole families who have come to Christ through a neighborhood witness that started when the TV was blaring, the baby was crying, children were fighting, or the man of the house was guzzling beer. "Perfect opportunities" seem to come along once in a while, but not often. The farmer who is forever uptight about the weather, the wind, and the clouds will sow little and reap less. So don't let the devil quiet you by suggesting "the time is not right"; it rarely is. But God has a way of overruling circumstances and blessing His Word regardless of the surroundings.

A second obstacle that keeps us from telling others about Jesus is fear: fear of failure, fear of offending, fear of losing a friend, fear of stirring up a rumpus, fear that we won't have all the answers, fear that we will be called "religious fanatics." The list is almost endless.

The Bible teaches that Christians are to be controlled by one Force: God. "Submit yourselves therefore to God" (James 4:7).

I have met a few absolutely fearless men, but they were almost abnormal. Most of us will feel some fear when it comes to witnessing. To this day, for example, I find that when I turn to a seatmate on a plane and attempt to engage him in a meaningful conversation about the Lord, my palms get wet, my throat gets dry, and my heart begins to beat faster.

As an encouragement to me many years ago, the Lord impressed on my mind the truth of 1 Peter 3:15: "But sanctify the Lord God in your hearts and be ready always to give an answer to every man that asketh you a reason of the hope that is in you with meekness and fear." *Meekness and fear!* Not brashness and glibness. Not with clever phrase-making!

However, though most of us *have* fear, we must not be *controlled* by fear. We are to be controlled by God and His power.

I was once going from Idaho to Nebraska on a furlough. The train stopped in Billings, Mont. about 3 A.M. With a couple of hours layover facing me, I went out on the streets to look around. I was not a Christian then and I looked for an open bar or some other action to kill the time.

Suddenly I heard a voice from half way down the block on a rather dimly lit street, "Hey, Marine!" I looked and saw a Royal Canadian Air Force officer surrounded by a half dozen threatening guys, one with a knife. The officer was motioning for me to come and give him a hand—and from the looks of things he needed it. I'm no hero. I wanted to run. The last thing I wanted to do was to head down that dark street at 3 A.M. and get in a fight with a half dozen guys.

But I couldn't leave. The Marines had instilled in me a pride in the Corps. And I thought that if that flyer made it back to Canada he would tell the story of the night he called on a chicken-hearted marine who refused to help. Somehow I couldn't let that happen.

So I started down the street, knees shaking and scared out of my wits. Fortunately, it was dark and the guys couldn't see how skinny and how frightened I was. They didn't know I hadn't the faintest idea what I was going to do.

Marine uniforms in those days included a wide, black leather belt with a heavy brass buckle. As I approached the group of men, I took off my belt, wrapped it around my hand a couple of times, and zeroed on the apparent leader carrying the knife. Stopping in front of him, I stood on my tiptoes to appear a little larger and waved my belt under his nose. My free hand jabbed at the knife, and I said in the deepest voice I could muster: "Have you ever eaten one of those things?" My heart pounded like a trip-hammer as I waited to see what would happen. To be honest, I thought I was going to faint! But my antagonist folded up his knife, stepped back, and the six of them walked off.

I had been afraid then, terribly afraid, but I was controlled by a force greater than my fear: a desire to maintain the honor of the Marine Corps. Consequently, fear had not paralyzed me.

As most of us experience some fear concerning witnessing, we need to realize that God has given us the Spirit "of power, and of love, and of a sound mind," not the spirit of fear (2 Tim. 1:7). You and I can give an answer to everyone that asks us a reason of the hope that is in us in the power of the Spirit.

You Have to Be Something

The third necessity for a good witness is that his life backs up what he says. As in the courtroom scene described earlier, the testimony of a known liar or self-promoter is a joke or worse.

A holy life is a sharp tool in the hands of a holy God. The Scriptures say, "Having therefore these promises, dearly beloved, let us cleanse ourselves from all filthiness of the flesh and spirit, perfecting holiness in the fear of God" (2 Cor. 7:1).

There are two rules in Romans 16:19 for spiritual health and the perfecting of holiness: "For your obedience is come abroad unto all men. I am glad therefore on your behalf; but yet I would have you wise unto that which is good, and simple concerning evil."

1. Be wise regarding good or righteous things.
2. Be simple—or ignorant—concerning evil.

The Apostle Paul uses a word here that has a reference to metal. "Simple" comes from the word "unmixed." Some metals are mixed, such as bronze and steel. Other metals are unmixed or pure, such as gold or silver. Paul encourages us to be unmixed regarding evil. Some Bible scholars use the word "innocent."

This has strong implications for what we read and what we see. Your eye is a camera that makes lasting impressions in your brain. What kind of pictures are stored there—collected from magazines, perhaps from movies, or from your own imaginings?

The Scriptures teach, "Brethren, whatsoever things are true, whatsoever things are honest, whatsoever things are just, whatsoever things are pure, whatsoever things are lovely, whatsoever things are of good report—if there be any virtue, and if there be any praise, think on these things" (Phil. 4:8).

God spoke to me from Genesis 1:4: "And God saw the light, that it was good, and God divided the light from the darkness." As God separated light from darkness at creation, that is His desire for my spiritual life.

John wrote: "This then is the message which we have heard of Him, and declare unto you, that God is light, and in Him is no darkness at all. If we say that we have fellowship with Him, and walk in darkness, we lie, and do not the truth; but if we walk in the light, as He is in the light, we have fellowship one with another, and the blood of Jesus Christ His Son cleanseth us from all sin" (1 John 1:5-7).

In heaven there is "no darkness at all," and in hell there is no light; it is a place of "outer darkness." As a Christian I will be living in heavenly light throughout eternity, so I should prepare myself here on earth.

Paul wrote: "If a man therefore purge himself from these [the unclean], he shall be a vessel unto honor, sanctified, and meet for the Master's use, and prepared unto every good work" (2 Tim. 2:21).

A clean vessel—body and soul—is fit for the Master's use. The super-talented, the extrovert, the guy with the gift of gab may or may not be a clean Christian. But the Christian with a holy life is the usable vessel, and this is something *we can change*.

Paul was chosen by the Lord and directed by Ananias to carry Christ's name into the world. "The Lord said unto [Ananias], 'Go thy way, for he is a chosen vessel unto Me, to bear My name before the Gentiles, and kings, and the children of Israel' "

(Acts 9:15). We also bear Jesus' name before the world by what we say, what we do, and what we are.

What we *are* carries the most impact by far, but God calls on us to *speak* His name and message for a very good reason.

A Christian businessman in Seattle confessed how he had unknowingly discouraged a business associate from coming to Christ for years. One day the friend told the Christian businessman he had met the Lord the night before through a Billy Graham meeting. The long-time Christian was elated and said so, but the new Christian replied, "Friend, you're the reason I have resisted becoming a Christian all these years. I figured that if a person could live a good life as you do and not be a Christian, there was no need to become one!" This Christian businessman had lived an exemplary life but he had not revealed the Source of strength for living it. Immediately he asked the Lord's forgiveness and His help to tell what and whom he knew that made the difference.

Here is God's tremendous promise to the people of Israel—and to His followers today—who choose His holy life: " 'And I will sanctify My great name, which was profaned among the heathen, which ye have profaned in the midst of them; and the heathen shall know that I am the Lord,' saith the Lord God, 'when I shall be sanctified in you before their eyes' " (Ezek. 36:23).

4

QUESTIONS—
AND ANSWERS

How do I bring Christ into casual conversations? How can I capitalize on the spiritual interest I sense in others? Is there a method for launching easily into any witnessing opportunity?

If you have questions like these about getting into a witnessing situation, you're in good company. Some of the best witnesses for Christ have difficulty getting started. But they still give a witness, and you can too. Here are three practical suggestions to help.

Make Friends

Develop friendships with non-Christians. Some Christians hardly know their neighbors well enough to talk about more than the weather. Invite acquaintances over for a barbecue or homemade ice cream. Take them to sporting events. Have a parlor-game night. When you have non-Christians in your home, keep some ash trays handy in case they smoke. Otherwise, a home can project the notion that the Bible teaches, "Give up smoking, believe on the Lord Jesus Christ, and thou shalt be saved."

The Bible doesn't teach that. Salvation is by faith, not works. Do what you can to make your friends feel at ease.

If non-Christians enjoy being around you, that indicates they will like the company of the Lord Jesus Christ—if we're representing Him. Remember the appeal of Jesus: "Then drew near unto Him all the publicans and sinners for to hear Him. And the Pharisees and scribes murmured, saying, 'This man receiveth sinners, and eateth with them'" (Luke 15:1-2).

Though scandalous to the self-righteous Pharisees, Jesus' mingling with disreputable people was an occasion for transforming lives. Remember the story of Zaccheus, the wealthy publican? "Jesus . . . looked up . . . and said unto him, 'Zaccheus, make haste . . . , for today I must abide at thy house.' And he made haste, and came down, and received Him joyfully. And when they saw it, they all murmured, saying that He was gone to be guest with a man that is a sinner. And Zaccheus stood, and said unto the Lord: 'Behold, Lord, the half of my goods I give to the poor; and if I have taken anything from any man by false accusation, I restore him fourfold'" (Luke 19:5-7).

Plan to go with your non-Christian friends to activities that they enjoy and which do not violate your conscience. If you have to decline attendance or participation on a spiritual principle, make clear you are not rejecting the people. You could say something like, "Sorry, we won't be able to make that, but we would like to get together with you. How about the school play next Friday night?" When you say no to an invitation this way, your friend sees that, though you didn't accept his invitation, you accept him. This is especially important when the friend may sense your personal disapproval of an activity. The *way* we express our standards and preferences speaks volumes to people with different views. Let me illustrate.

I don't smoke. Suppose a non-Christian buddy offers me a cigarette. "No, thanks, I don't smoke. I'm a Christian."

This friend doesn't really care whether I smoke or not. He just wants to be generous and friendly. If I say, "No thanks, I never picked up the habit," he may tell me how lucky I am and admit that he wishes he hadn't.

When you encounter a co-worker that you would like to win to Christ, focus first on winning his friendship as a *person*. Ask about his interests. Get involved in the things that interest him. As you show interest in his hobbies or pastimes, he will naturally become interested in the important things in your life. Quite possibly your interest in a guy's hot rod could lead to his interest in the Gospel. Friendship takes time, but this is true Christian love in action.

Real love for our "neighbor" may require sacrificial actions that demonstrate we care for the person's earthly welfare as well as his eternal soul. I unexpectedly found myself in such a situation in Reno, Nev.

I was traveling to Denver that winter day, and while waiting in the train depot, I saw two young men come in who were riding a freight train toward California. It was a bitterly cold day, and I knew the freight had to cross the high mountain pass on its way to Sacramento. The two of them were dressed in lightweight trousers and cotton shirts. I knew that within minutes I would be on a warm passenger train and that I had two overcoats with me. I was wearing one and the other was in my suitcase. The one in my suitcase was a gift from a service center director. It was a navy officer's wool topcoat that had been left at the center and never reclaimed.

The Holy Spirit brought the question to my mind: What would Jesus do? I asked one of the young men if he had a coat and he said no. I took off my overcoat and said, "Let's see if this fits you." I put it on him and it fit quite well.

The other guy was rather sullen, and I opened my suitcase, took out the wool topcoat, and said, "Here, try this one."

He replied, "I'm not cold."

I laughed. "You're not cold now, pal, but you will be when you start to cross that mountain pass in an unheated boxcar of a slow-moving freight." A flicker of a smile crossed his face and he tried on my coat. It fit perfectly. He walked over to the depot window and looked at himself in the reflector.

The first guy looked at me and said, "Why do you want to give us your coat?"

I laughed again. "A few years ago I sure wouldn't have done it, but something happened to me not too long ago that changed my whole attitude toward people."

"Oh yeah? What was that?" he asked.

I had the joy of telling him how Christ had come into my heart, changed my life, and given me a concern for people's needs. My train was leaving momentarily, but I had a Gospel booklet with me that I offered to them. They accepted it gladly and assured me they would read it.

I don't know what happened to those men, but I believe they were more willing to consider my

Christ because He had made me responsive to their needs.

Recently I heard about a Christian girl befriending a handicapped girl at a Midwestern university. The disabled student can write, speak, and get around in a motorized wheelchair, though everything takes her twice as long as for an average person. The Christian first helped Laura (not her real name) through a door one day and met her at the same place on succeeding days to lend a hand.

Discouraged with studies, Laura confided her difficulties, and her new Christian friend responded by describing ways God had been answering her own prayers about academic frustrations. That encouraged Laura to attend her church the next Sunday for the first time in many months.

Throughout the semester the friendship developed through all sorts of activities. Then the possibility loomed that Laura would have to drop out of school. She had stayed up most of the night studying for exams and her friend exclaimed, "Laura, I don't know what keeps you going." When Laura admitted she didn't know either, the friend said she wanted to show Laura something that kept her going.

It was the "Bridge," a sketch of a chasm with "Man" on one side and "God" on the other. When Laura was asked if she knew how to get from the land of Man to the land of God, she thought a minute and said, "You know. You tell me."

The Christian said that we experience a living death and frustration when we run our own lives, but when Christ runs our lives we experience joy and peace and life in the "land of God." Laura said she felt halfway across the bridge and wanted

to go over completely with Christ as her Lord.
They prayed together, and only then did Laura
reveal that she had been reading the New Testament in a modern-language version. Laura's school
situation is uncertain at the moment, but her future
is securely in God's hands.

Ask Questions

The second suggestion for creating witnessing opportunities is: learn to ask questions that will lead
to a spiritual discussion. A few personal experiences
will show what I mean.

One summer while driving from North Platte,
Nebr. to Colorado Springs, I picked up a hitchhiker
just outside a small town. Driving through the
town, I commented that there were a lot of churches
for a town so small. He agreed. I asked, "Do you
go to church much?"

"Nah—I used to, but not any more."

"Did your church talk much about heaven?"

"Yeh, some."

"What do you think it's like?"

"Pretty nice, I guess."

"Do you think heaven is going to be perfect?"

"Yep. And I guess it's about the only place that
is."

"Well now, let me ask you another question. When
you think of your life, do you think it's perfect or
imperfect?"

"Well, sir, it ain't perfect."

I laughed. "Mine's not either." Then I asked,
"When you die, would you like to go to heaven?"

"I don't think about it much, but I guess so."

"Well then, that poses a problem. Because if God
let you into heaven like you are, heaven would no
longer be perfect, because you'd be there, and like

you say, you're not perfect."

He smiled. "I never thought of it that way."

"So then God either has to change you or change heaven, and I suppose heaven is pretty set in its ways by now. How do you think a person can change his ways and get good enough for heaven? Have you ever tried to change—make New Year's resolutions, for instance?"

"Yeah, I tried them every year for a long time, but it didn't work. I don't seem to be able to keep 'em."

I agreed. "Most people can't."

I paused to let that sink in, then told him, "You know, the Bible tells a way to change so that anyone can start out fresh and clean with a life that God accepts." I shared 2 Corinthians 5:17, "Therefore if any man be in Christ, he is a new creature; old things are passed away; behold, all things are become new."

I then offered: "Let me tell you how it happened to me." I gave him my personal testimony and followed with Scripture verses that explained the Gospel. We arrived at his town before I was able to try to lead him to a decision, but he took a piece of Christian literature and said he'd read it.

That series of questions has proved helpful for me on quite a few occasions.

1. *Do you think heaven is a perfect place?*

2. *How close have you come to a perfect life?*

3. *If God lets you go to heaven as you are, what will happen to heaven's perfect record?*

4. *Do you see any hope in the Bible verse— 2 Corinthians 5:17?*

A friend of mine uses the following question effectively:

"Bill, if you die and go up to the pearly gates

and knock, and the Lord answers and says, 'Why should I let you into My heaven?' what would you tell Him?"

There are only two basic answers to that question: one involves faith, and the other a good life. Usually the person will come up with an answer that is based on some sort of "good works"— church membership, baptism, donations to charities, being a good husband or faithful wife, or performing kind acts to people in need. But the Bible is very clear on the works-faith issue. I encourage you to memorize and use these two verses: "By grace are ye saved through faith; and that not of yourselves; it is the gift of God, not of works, lest any man should boast" (Eph. 2:8-9).

I might comment after quoting these verses: "Suppose we all get to heaven and I go around bragging, 'You should have seen what I did to get here. I was the neighborhood "old reliable," paid my bills, always voted, coached in Little League, and always rewarded the paper boy at Christmas!' Would that kind of boasting make heaven pleasant for you? No, it would be the same old stuff we've suffered down here. Salvation is 'not of works, lest any man should boast.'"

Titus 3:5-7 is another helpful passage on the futility of seeking acceptance because of good works. "Not by works of righteousness which we have done, but according to His mercy He saved us, by the washing of regeneration, and renewing of the Holy Ghost; which He shed on us abundantly through Jesus Christ our Saviour; that being justified by His grace, we should be made heirs according to the hope of eternal life."

Clearly, entrance into heaven is "not by works." But we note the value of "good works" for Christians in Titus 3:8, "This is a faithful saying, and these things I will that thou affirm constantly, that they which have believed in God might be careful to maintain good works. These things are good and profitable unto men." Genuine good works are a *result* of salvation—not the means to gain salvation.

"*So you have an interest in religious things?*" This question begins another series that many people have found helpful. Imagine Diane and Brenda in conversation. There has been a casual reference to religion or church, and Diane asks, "By the way, do you have much interest in spiritual things, Brenda?"

"No," Brenda says.

The beauty of this question is that Brenda may say yes or no without derailing the questioner. Only the emphasis is changed in the next question.

Since Brenda's answer was "No," Diane asks, "Tell me, Brenda, have you *ever* considered becoming a real Christian?" (emphasizing the possibility of a decision sometime in the past) If Brenda had said, "Yes," Diane could have asked, "Tell me, have you ever considered becoming a *real* Christian?" (emphasizing *real*—that is, a dedicated follower of Christ)

Whether Brenda answers "No" or "Yes," Diane's next question is the same: "Tell me, Brenda, if someone were to ask you what a real Christian is, what would you say?"

Here we come again to only two possible answers: faith in God or meritorious works. If Brenda answers something that relates to good works, Diane would say, "I agree that a real Christian *does* those things, but what *is* a real Christian? How does a person become one?"

If Brenda is unsure at this point, Diane can take

her Bible and say, "Let me show you a few Bible verses that really cleared the matter up for me."

However, if Brenda says something that relates to faith, such as "Believe in Jesus," Diane would say, "Exactly! Let me tell you how it happened to me." At that point she would give her personal testimony or show Brenda the Gospel in the Scriptures. Either of these could be used to clarify the Gospel message to Brenda.

"If someone were to ask you . . ." Involving an imagined third person is a very helpful aspect in such a question. This doesn't put a person in an uncomfortable spot as much as a direct question.

Depending on Brenda's reaction, Diane may confront her with a decision: "Brenda, do you know any reason why you wouldn't want to invite Jesus into your heart right now and become a real Christian?"

To review these questions quickly, they are:

1. "Are you interested in spiritual things?"

2. "Have you ever considered becoming a real Christian?"

3. "If someone were to ask you what is a real Christian, what would you tell them?"

4. "Do you know any reason why you wouldn't want to invite Jesus into your heart right now and become a real Christian?"

Another series of questions is helpful if your friend has attended church or evangelistic services where he heard the Gospel.

Put those questions in this setting and consider a few clarifying ideas.

Mr. Green and Mr. Jones have attended church.

Let's suppose Mr. Jones invited Mr. Green to go to his church, since the Greens were new in the neighborhood. Sometime later Mr. Jones sees Mr.

Green and asks, "What did you think of the sermon Sunday?"

Mr. Green is too polite to say anything derogatory about the service, so he answers, "It was fine."

"Did you have any questions about what the preacher said?" asks the Christian.

Perhaps Mr. Green didn't understand it, but he may be too proud to admit it, so he says, "No, it was very clear." If he should say he didn't understand, Mr. Jones could explain the Gospel and give his own testimony.

But since Mr. Green says it was clear, Mr. Jones can say, "Tell me, Mr. Green, do you know God personally, or are you still on the way?"

"Well, I guess I am still on the way," Mr. Green concedes.

"I sure understand that," Mr. Jones says sympathetically. "It wasn't until a few years ago that I took the step of commitment." And at that point Mr. Jones gives his testimony. When Mr. Green seems to understand, he asks, "Would you want to invite the Lord into your heart right now?"

The phrase ". . . or are you still on the way?" is a very tactful line for Mr. Jones to include because it is considerate of Mr. Green's feelings and it adds a positive note to the discussion.

What is your work?" begins another set of questions for men meeting briefly and casually.

Bob turns to his seatmate on the plane, and the two engage in light conversation. After a while Bob asks, "Harry, what is your work (or business)?"

"I'm in the insurance business."

"Is that so? Tell me, how did you decide on that field?"

"Oh, I had an uncle who had been in insurance for years and he offered to help get me started, so it was a natural for someone who had no other plans."

"Harry, what principles or guidelines can help a young man decide what to do with his life?"

"Well, aptitude and interests have a lot to do with it, but I suppose intelligence to recognize a good opportunity is important."

"That's surely right. You know, something happened a few years ago that added a whole new dimension to my answer to that question."

"Oh, yes? What was that?"

"Well, I'm in the building business, but some years ago I decided that I was going to give my life to helping meet the real needs of the world. As a contractor I can provide houses for people and office buildings and sites for stores and the like. And I do that. But the thing I've come to believe is that the real needs of the world are spiritual. We need to come up with a solution to the hate and greed, murder and wars, and general turmoil that dominates the news. Four years ago I became a Christian —a follower of Christ. There is a Bible verse that says, 'Therefore, if any man be in Christ he is a new creature; old things are passed away; behold, all things are become new.'

"In order to change the world, we must change people, because people make up society. And there is one power that brings a deep moral change into the lives of people. That power is God. The way it happened to me, Harry, is interesting. . . ." At that point Bob gives his testimony to Harry.

And, of course, a Christian in a different vocation can adapt this approach to fit his or her specialty.

Find the Open Nerve
A third way to develop witness opportunities in

addition to making friendships and asking leading questions is to look for the "open" or exposed nerve in a dialogue. Witnessing can be compared to climbing a mountain. Some mountains can be climbed with ease; there are paths directly to the peaks. Other mountains are extremely difficult to scale. One route is tried, then another. One path is blocked by a rock slide, another by a sheer cliff and high winds. Persistence will uncover a route that leads to the peak and the summit is conquered. We are to be ready for either type of advance.

Once while flying from Dallas to Colorado Springs, I found my seatmate to be a young soldier going home to Oklahoma City. Nervous and a bit dejected, he revealed his problem. His friends and family had had a big celebration for him when he entered the service, and now, a few weeks later, he was going home, medically discharged. The Army discovered a physical problem that made him unfit for active duty and he was unsure how his friends and family would react.

As we talked, I saw that he was eager to discuss spiritual realities. He admitted he needed Christ in his life, and as the plane touched down at Oklahoma City he bowed his head to ask Christ into his life. His greatest need had been recognized and met.

A few weeks later I boarded a plane for Chicago and sat next to a man wearing white trousers, a purple silk shirt, a scarf about his neck, and large sunglasses. I thought to myself, *He looks like a movie producer.* Sure enough! He said he was a movie producer. As we talked, I steered the conversation to spiritual matters. Though he was willing to talk, he was not seriously interested. When the conversation became personal, he brought up objections and difficulties he had with the Bible. When

I gave him straightforward answers, he veered the conversation into other directions.

We parted on a cordial note, but this flight companion was apparently no closer to the kingdom of God than when I began witnessing. I could not find an "exposed nerve" that pained the man enough to seek healing.

When you go to a dentist and he begins to probe, nothing happens at first. He touches this tooth and that one and all of a sudden—whammo—you shoot upward! He has struck a tender nerve, and you two are in business!

There are a number of raw nerves in contemporary society that make people sensitive to the Gospel.

1. *Boredom with life.* Much of our society is bored stiff. Millions follow a dull routine that gives no challenge or variety. In the New Testament, life was often unpredictable and exciting for Jesus' followers.

But Jesus Christ adds a zest and vigor to ordinary life today. He plainly declared: "I am come that they might have life, and that they might have it more abundantly" (John 10:10). The Christian witness who expresses this joyous life will find bored moderns looking curiously for the cause.

2. *Deep meaninglessness.* Many people get up in the morning under a dark cloud of futility. They expect to find no pleasure in their pastimes. They have no serious goals in life, and they are plagued with a sense of triviality in everything. They crave something but don't know what it is. There is a nameless nostalgia in their souls. These people are not awakened to God and they are incomplete.

The Bible says, "Beware lest any man spoil you through philosophy and vain deceit, after the tradition of men, after the rudiments of the world, and not after Christ. For in Him dwelleth all the fullness of the Godhead bodily. And ye are complete in Him, which is the head of all principality and power" (Col. 2:8-10).

A person becomes complete when he is united spiritually with his Creator through faith in Christ. A Christian is involved in the noblest venture open to humans: discovering the will of God for his life. He is guided by Romans 12:2, "And be not conformed to this world; but be ye transformed by the renewing of your mind, that ye may prove what is that good, and acceptable, and perfect will of God." This gives meaning to all of life!

3. *Crippling guilt.* This raw nerve is covered by layers of excuses, pride, anger, and repressed memories. It is one of the greatest afflictions of our time, but often it is unrecognized. The victims sometimes try false helpers such as alcohol or drugs and get temporary relief. God's forgiveness and love are the cure for this widespread malady.

A young man once told me, "I'd give anything to feel clean inside." Jesus offers just that, as the Apostle John testified: "Jesus Christ . . . loved us, and washed us from our sins in His own blood" (Rev. 1:5).

4. *Aching loneliness.* I know people who are convinced that no one cares whether they live or die. I've heard of a person who stays up every night until the TV station signs off just so he will hear someone say goodnight to him. Loneliness is miserable. Jesus Christ offers a double answer to loneliness: He offers fellowship with other members of the family of God and "body" of Christ; He offers His own gracious presence: "I will never leave thee nor forsake thee" (Heb. 13:5).

5. *Fear of death*. This is a worldwide malady. A Japanese college sophomore told me that he went to bed every night fearing what might confront him if he didn't wake up. Twelve other students nodded in agreement with his statement. That marvelously changed when the student entrusted his life to the Lord of time and eternity!

"These things have I written unto you that believe on the Son of God," wrote John, "that ye may know that ye have eternal life" (1 John 5:13). This assurance is part of Christ's gift of salvation. John elaborates: "And this is the record, that God hath given to us eternal life, and this life is in His Son. He that hath the Son hath life, and he that hath not the Son of God hath not life" (1 John 5:11-12).

God will give you wisdom and grace for approaching strangers and making friendships in order to communicate God's answers to the biggest questions in life.

5

PERSON TO PERSON

One could tell by the way he spoke that he was a well-educated man, and yet he did not know how to come to God. He said, "Our priest repeatedly emphasizes that we should come to Christ, but my question is, precisely how does one do that?" He knew what he was supposed to do, but did not know how to do it.

Acceptance by God is a mystery both to the man paddling down the Amazon River hunting jaguar and the man speeding along Interstate 80 in his Jaguar. Neither of these travelers will know the love, forgiveness, and eternal salvation of God unless he is told by us who know Him.

This sacred mission for God is described by Paul in 2 Corinthians 5:18, 20. "God . . . hath reconciled us to Himself by Jesus Christ, and hath given to us the ministry of reconciliation. . . . Now then we are ambassadors for Christ. . . ."

What are the basic facts of the reconciling Gospel? Paul gives them in 1 Corinthians 15:1-4. "Moreover, brethren, I declare unto you the Gospel which I preached unto you, which also ye have received, and wherein ye stand. . . . For I delivered unto you first of all that which I also received, how that Christ died for our sins according to the Scriptures; and that He was buried, and that He rose again the third day according to the Scriptures."

1. Christ died for our sins.
2. He was buried.
3. He rose again—conqueror over death and sin.

Charlie and Ned Discuss the Way to God

A hypothetical conversation between Charlie the Christian and Ned the non-Christian will show how to use some Scriptures pointing the way to reconciliation with God.

The two friends have been "talking religion" for quite a while when Charlie says, "Ned, there are a few verses in the Bible that I know you would find interesting and helpful along these lines. Would you like to see them?"

"OK."

Charlie opens his Bible to Romans 3:23 and hands the book to Ned. "Read the 23rd verse."

" 'For all have sinned, and come short of the glory of God.' "

"Ned, here's the main truth of that verse: nobody's perfect. We're all in the same boat when it comes to sinning against God. You've sinned. I've sinned. Does that make sense to you?"

Ned thinks for a moment. "Yep, I can vouch for that."

"Now, let's look at Romans 6:23. Read this one."

" 'For the wages of sin is death, but the gift of God is eternal life through Jesus Christ our Lord.' "

"We're going to get paid for our life-work, Ned, and the wages for our sins is *death!* I heard our pastor say once that the word death means 'separation.' And it makes sense that sin would separate. For instance, suppose Joe, a businessman, comes to work one morning and finds the safe open and all the cash and negotiable stocks and bonds gone. He sees a note from Jake, his business partner, which says, 'So long, sucker. I've gone to Bolivia.' Somehow there isn't the warmth in his heart for old Jake that there once was. What's happened? Jake has sinned against Joe, and now there's a severance of their relationship. Sin always separates.

"Or, suppose a man sins against his wife? There's an estrangement in their relationship. Maybe not in the legal sense, but certainly in their communication. You can feel it in the air. Does that show how sin causes separation from God?"

"Yes, I think so."

"OK. Let's look next at Hebrews 9:27. Here it is."

Ned takes the Bible and reads aloud: " 'It is appointed unto men once to die, but after this the judgment.' "

Ned looks up and protests: "I thought you said the Gospel was *good news*. I don't see any good news here. One verse says we've all sinned; another says we're separated from God because of sin; and this one says we are all going to face the judgment of God. Where's the good news in that?"

"That part makes the Good News all the better, Ned. Sin has to be paid for, God says, so we have to look for the payment that will spare us from death. Suppose you are hauled in front of a judge for a traffic fine. You say if he'll forget it you will promise never to do it again. Will he let you go?"

"Probably not."

"That's the way it is with God too. We have violated His law, and a penalty must be paid for that violation. That fact is definitely not good news, but it can lead us to the Good News. For example, read this in Romans 5:8."

Again Ned takes the Bible and reads: " 'But God commendeth His love toward us, in that, while we were yet sinners, Christ died for us.' "

"Ned, this is one of the most exciting verses in the whole Bible. Suppose you had to pay a $100 fine to that judge I mentioned. He could help you, if you couldn't pay, by stepping down beside you and paying the penalty himself!"

Ned begins to understand. "What you are saying is that Christ did that for me. He paid the penalty for my sins, and now I don't have to!"

"That's right! God has said His salvation is a free gift. Read this verse." Charlie points to Ephesians 2:8-9.

" 'For by grace are ye saved through faith; and that not of yourselves; it is the gift of God: not of works, lest any man should boast.' "

"Like any gift, Ned, this one must be received to be enjoyed. That's the point of this next verse, John 1:12."

Ned reads the passage: " 'But as many as received Him, to them gave He power to become the sons of God, even to them that believe on His name.' "

"Let's think this through, Ned. First, what must be believed?"

Ned ponders a moment. "I must believe on His name."

"Right. And what must be received?"

"I must receive *Him*."

"This chapter is talking about Jesus Christ, so we must receive Him into our lives. Now, the big question: If I receive Christ, what do I become?"

The realization hits Ned. "*A son of God!*"

"Right! Isn't that great?"

"Great is hardly the word for it. It seems too simple . . . or too impossible . . . or too good to be true!"

"It seemed that way to me, too, at first. Then I realized that God meant exactly what He said. Do you know how to receive Christ?"

"I don't understand how you can receive a *person*, but I suppose it has to do with saying a prayer."

"Another verse, Revelation 3:20, will help make it clear. Read this."

"'Behold, I stand at the door and knock; if any man hear My voice, and open the door, I will come in to Him, and will sup with him, and he with Me.'"

"This is Christ speaking, Ned. He is knocking at the door of your heart and asking to come into your life. You 'open the door' by asking Him to come in as your Saviour and Lord. When you do, He promises to enter and fellowship with you as a friend. Do you want to be a son of God?"

"Yes, but I don't know what to say."

Charlie takes out a piece of paper and says, "I think this will help. These are Jesus' words in John 14:14, '"If ye shall ask anything in My name, I will do it."'"

"What would you like Jesus Christ to do for you, Ned?"

"Well, I know I need Him to forgive my sins."

"Let's put that down on the paper." He writes, "I accept Your forgiveness for my sins."

"What else, Ned?"

"I want Him to come into my heart."

"We'll write that down also. Anything else?"

"I remember your saying that Jesus is your personal Saviour and Lord—I want Him for my Lord and Saviour too."

"Great. We'll put that down. Anything more?"

"No, I can't think of anything."

"How about asking Him to be your Guide from this day on?"

"OK."

The paper now looks like this:

"If ye shall ask anything in My name, I will do it" (John 14:14).

1. *Lord, please forgive my sins.*
2. *Jesus, please come into my heart.*
3. *Lord Jesus, please be my personal Saviour and Lord.*
4. *Jesus, please be my Guide from this day on.*

Charlie hands the paper to Ned. "You can ask for these right now, or if you prefer you can wait until you are alone. Whatever you wish."

Ned takes the paper. "I want to do it right now. There's no use putting it off any longer."

"Do you want to pray aloud or silently, just between you and God?"

"I think I'd rather pray silently."

"OK. When you've finished, say amen out loud and then I'll pray."

Ned bows his head and prays silently for a few moments and then says amen. Charlie prays aloud and thanks the Lord for dying on the cross for their sin and for coming into their hearts and living there. Afterward he asks: "Well, Ned, where is Jesus right now?"

Ned looks perplexed, then smiles broadly. *"In my heart!"*

"How do you know that for sure?"

"I asked Him in, and He said He would come."

"Right. Let's look at one more passage: 1 John 5:11-12." Charlie reads it: " 'And this is the record, that God hath given to us eternal life, and this life is in His Son. He that hath the Son hath life, and he that hath not the Son of God hath not life.'

"Here's a great promise, Ned. Because you have the Son of God in your life, what else do you have?"

"The verse says I have eternal life."

"Right. I suggest you memorize that verse before the day is over. It will give you assurance in the days ahead."

This imaginary discussion suggests how you can share key verses so they can be understood by a person who needs to make a decision for Christ. If you have no other plan to follow, I suggest that you memorize each of the verses so you can readily lead a seeking person through them. The series and their points are:

Romans 3:23—All have sinned.

Romans 6:23—Penalty for sin.

Hebrews 9:27—Penalty must be paid.

Romans 5:8—Penalty paid by Christ.

Ephesians 2:8-9—Salvation a free gift.

John 1:12—Must receive Christ.

Revelation 3:20—Christ at heart's door.

1 John 5:11-12—Assurance of salvation.

The encounter between "Charlie" and "Ned" is not a pattern of witnessing for every situation. No two situations are exactly alike. Yet this series of verses form a clear path which an inexperienced witness can easily remember. As experience is gained, additional verses will help meet the varied needs of people.

Each of Jesus' opportunities was unique and each of the apostles' opportunities was set in a different framework. At times they found eager, responsive people and at times they found quite the opposite. In all cases, God's Word was the instrument used to enlighten and convict—or condemn.

In my witnessing I have found two major problems rising again and again: What does it mean to repent? How could Jesus be both God and man?

True Repentance

When a person makes a decision for Christ, he may or may not express deep emotions. Some people think great remorse for sins equals the true repentance of which Jesus spoke: "'Except ye repent, ye shall all likewise perish'" (Luke 13:3). Repentance actually means a change of mind or change of direction, which may or may not involve strong feelings.

Imagine you are driving down the road of life and you see Jesus Christ standing beside a crossroad, waiting for an invitation to travel with you. If you stop your car, reach back, and open the back door for Him, you shouldn't expect Him to enter. Nor if you lean over and open the door for Him to sit beside you would He respond. Only as you slide over and invite Him to take the steering wheel will this Traveler come in. This illustrates true repentance! Acknowledging that Jesus Christ is your Lord and turning over your way to His direction and control is the repentance Jesus asks.

This truth is illuminated by the royal reality that a believer is born into the kingdom of God— becoming a loyal subject of Jesus Christ, our King of kings and Lord of lords.

Another clear picture of repentance is given in 1 Thessalonians 1:5, 9-10 "For our Gospel did not come to you in word only, but also in power and in the Holy Spirit and with full conviction . . . and . . . you turned to God from idols to serve a living and true God, and to wait for His Son from heaven, whom He raised from the dead, that is Jesus, who delivers us from the wrath to come" (NASB).

The people of Thessalonica who read this letter from Paul became followers of the Lord: they turned *to* God *from* idols to serve their new Master.

They turned to God—for salvation.

They turned away from idols—for purity.

They determined to serve—in loving submission.

Jesus Is Both Divine and Human

The Scriptures declare that Jesus is God and also a man. "Paul, a bond-servant of Christ Jesus, called as an apostle, set apart for the Gospel of God, which He promised beforehand through His prophets in the holy Scriptures, concerning His Son, who was born of the seed of David according to the flesh, who was declared with power to be the Son of God by the resurrection from the dead, according to the Spirit of holiness, Jesus Christ our Lord." (Rom. 1:1-4, NASB)

Here the Apostle Paul affirms Jesus' human nature in the words, "born of the seed of David according to the flesh." His divine nature is established by the words, "declared to be the Son of God."

Isaiah focuses additional light on this mystery. "For unto us a Child is born, unto us a Son is given; and the government shall be upon His shoulder; and His name shall be called Wonderful, Counselor, the mighty God, the everlasting Father, the Prince of Peace" (9:6). Notice that "a Child is *born,* a Son is *given.*" The human child was born at Bethlehem, and God gave his own Son in that birth.

Centuries before Jesus' birth, Isaiah predicted: "Behold, a virgin shall conceive, and bear a Son, and shall call His name Immanuel" (7:14). Comparing this with Matthew 1:23, we read the angel's announcement to Joseph: "Behold, a virgin shall be with Child, and shall bring forth a Son, and they shall call His name Emmanuel, which being interpreted is, 'God with us.'"

That prophecy was fulfilled in Jesus' birth to Mary. Jesus had a human mother—but His only Father was Jehovah! So the Man born in a humble stable is also the mighty God! We don't need to fully understand this, but we can believe it by God's gift of faith.

A naturalist observing a colony of ants in a field noticed that they would scurry to their holes when his shadow fell over the ant hill. Impulsively he wished he could convey to them his peaceful intentions, but realized that would be possible only if he became an ant like they were.

His situation was similar to God's lofty eminence over creation. In order to walk and talk with humanity, Jesus came to this earth and led the way through life and death back to the Father, who loves us and yearns for our fellowship.

Anthropologists are on an endless search for the "missing link" between apes and men. One author suggested that a more noble search would be to find the link between men and God. Such a "link" would be both human and divine. We thank God that the "link" is already revealed in the Scriptures as Jesus Christ, Immanuel—God with us. This grand search has ended for everyone who believes Jesus' words: "I and My Father are one" (John 10:30).

As a new Christian, I gained courage and experience for witnessing by teaming up with a friend. We practiced giving each other the message of the Gospel. We shared verses and illustrations that made the message clear. I recommend this practice to you.

6

SHARPENED TOOLS

"What I need is some sort of a plan to help me make the Gospel more understandable. I want some handy tools to use in the difficult cases."

I've heard that said many times and I reply, "Possibly. But I assure you that effective witnessing is not a matter of memorizing plans or mastering gimmicks. Fruitfulness in witnessing is a product of a Christian's close walk with Jesus and of the Holy Spirit's conviction of the sinner. I can follow a plan, but I must rely on the Lord."

A plan or tool can help you get started in witnessing, and it can clarify the way of salvation to doubters. The illustration-tools in this chapter have been effectively used by many witnesses.

Arrow of History and the Intellectual

Two men are business associates in a large office building. One of them reads a lot, and lately he has been pondering some rather difficult philosophical questions. Why is there evil in the world? If God is all-powerful, why doesn't He restrain evil forces? Why does history seem to be full of wars and strife?

He has talked about these questions to a Christian friend, Al Stephens. One day at the cafeteria on their lunch hour together, Al brings up these important issues.

"Frank, I've been thinking about those questions we were discussing the other day, and I ran across an illustration that pretty well explains them for me. Would you like to see it?"

Frank looks at his watch and says, "Sure, Al, if it won't take too long. You know I've got to get those reports out this afternoon, and I want to get back fairly soon."

"OK, Frank," Al replies. "This won't take too long, and I think you'll enjoy seeing it."

"Recorded History"

Al takes an envelope from his coat pocket and draws an arrow on the back. "Let's say this arrow represents the entire course of time." He then sections off a portion in the middle where he writes "Recorded History."

RECORDED HISTORY

"Frank," continues Al, "what would you say characterizes history as you remember it from your reading and studies in school?"

"Well," says Frank, "it is full of war and social injustices and powerful people riding roughshod over the ordinary guy. It seems we pinpoint events by dating them either before or after a war. History hasn't been all that pleasant."

"That's the way I remember it, too," says Al. "Let me jot this down under recorded history." Al writes "strife, war, man's inhumanity to man."

The paper now looks like this:

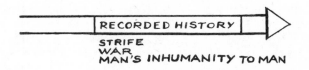

RECORDED HISTORY

STRIFE
WAR
MAN'S INHUMANITY TO MAN

He then turns to Frank and says, "I'm reminded of the statements of a couple of world-renowned thinkers and leaders. They sort of summarize our history. British dramatist George Bernard Shaw said, 'We are still savages at heart, and wear our thin uniform of civilization awkwardly.'

"French statesman Georges Clemenceau said, 'Perhaps man's history is simpler than we think. It is summed up in proclaiming the right and doing the wrong.'"

"Those sure say it clearly, don't they?" agrees Frank.

"Yes, and assuming that man is a product of his environment there is very little hope for improvement. As far back as we look there is nothing but man swashbuckling through history, leaving bloody tracks on every page. We can't see a sunny dawn for the world in the future, because today's newspaper is no more cheerful than last month's, or last year's."

Al paused at the solemn thought, then went on. "Yet I believe that God created the world. Last week I told a fellow that. He said, 'If God made this world, He must have a streak of evil in Him! How could a good God create a world full of strife and suffering and evil of every sort, unless God is the devil?'"

Frank says, "I've often wondered that very thing. It just doesn't make sense."

Al draws another arrow a few inches above the first one. "Frank, this next part helps clear up the mystery."

Above the top arrow Al writes, "The kind of life God intended," and in the arrow he writes the words, "love, peace, joy." Near the tail of the arrow he sections off a portion and writes, "moral choice."

The illustration now looks like this:

"Frank, let's look at a few Scriptures which indicate the kind of life God intended for us to live. Jesus taught that life should not be characterized by strife, but by love—for God and from God. He said, 'Thou shalt love the Lord thy God with all thy heart, and with all thy soul, and with all thy strength, and with all thy mind; and thy neighbor as thyself'" (Luke 10:27).

Frank smiles. "That sounds other-worldly. Are you sure that is meant for us?"

"It sure is," says Al. "The Bible also teaches that God not only intended us to be full of love, but of peace and joy as well. Look at these Scriptures.

" ' "Peace I leave with you, My peace I give unto you; not as the world giveth, give I unto you. Let not your heart be troubled, neither let it be afraid" ' (John 14:27).

" 'Thou wilt keep him in perfect peace, whose mind is stayed on Thee, because he trusteth in Thee' (Isa. 26:3).

" 'Therefore being justified by faith, we have peace with God through our Lord Jesus Christ' (Rom. 5:1).

" ' "Hitherto have ye asked nothing in My name; ask, and ye shall receive, that your joy may be full" ' (John 16:24).

" ' "These things have I spoken unto you, that My joy might remain in you, and that your joy might be full" ' (John 15:11)."

As Frank ponders these things, Al resumes his explanation. "In the beginning man had the capacity to live like this and he did, because God made man in His own image. Man was truthful and selfless, because God had given him these perfect characteristics. Along with a perfect moral nature, however, God gave man the choice of continuing in this way of life or stepping out of it. Harmony is not love if it is forced, and God longed for man to love Him voluntarily with his whole heart and mind and soul. So God gave man his choice—God's way or his own."

A glimmer of understanding flickers in Frank's eyes. "To put it simply, Frank, man blew it. He chose to do his own thing. The prophet Isaiah (53: 6) described it this way: 'All we like sheep have gone astray; we have turned everyone to his own way.' "

At this point Al draws a diagonal bar from "moral

choice" to "recorded history" and labels it "sin." He continues: "The essence of sin is man going his own way, away from God."

Now Al's illustration looks like this:

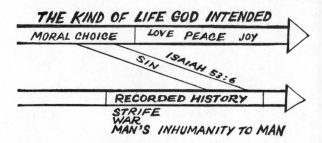

"Man, going his own way apart from God, has made a terrible mess of the world. There have always been reformers, poets, artists, authors, and statesmen who have struggled to elevate mankind, but they often fight a losing battle. We see the same thing today.

"But the thrilling message of Scripture is that God invaded human history by sending His own Son, Jesus Christ, from heaven to build the way back to the Godlike life of love. Consider these words of Jesus found in John 16:28-29, ' "I came forth from the Father and am come into the world; again, I leave the world and go to the Father." His disciples said unto Him, "Lo, now speakest Thou plainly and speakest no proverb." ' And in John 8:42—' "I proceeded forth and came from God; neither came I of Myself, but He sent Me." '

"Jesus is not man's best endeavor to find God; He is God's plan to reach men. John 14:6 quotes Jesus: 'I am the Way, the Truth, and the Life; no man cometh unto the Father, but by Me.'

"How is Christ the way back to God? How did He accomplish this? He did it by dying on the cross with the world's sins on His soul. As God and perfect Man, He could pay the penalty for others' sins. We see this in Romans 5:8, 'But God commendeth His love toward us, in that, while we were yet sinners, Christ died for us.' Also, 1 Peter 3:18 says, 'For Christ also hath once suffered for sins, the Just for the unjust, that He might bring us to God.'

"With the penalty for sin completely paid, any believer in Christ is restored to the life of love and peace and joy that God originally intended. He has Christ living within to give both intimate fellowship with God and strength to conquer evil. Jesus said, ' "I am come that they might have life, and that they might have it more abundantly" ' (John 10:10)."

Al now completes his illustration by drawing a cross between the two arrows, the completed illustration looking like this:

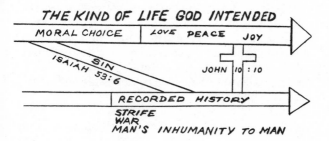

"The Apostle Paul put it this way: 'Therefore, if any man be in Christ, he is a new creature; old things are passed away; behold, all things are become new' (2 Cor. 5:17).

"In another passage, Paul wrote, 'Who [God] hath delivered us from the power of darkness, and hath translated us into the kingdom of His dear Son' (Col. 1:13).

"These three passages show that in Christ we can have life, become a new person, and be made a citizen of God's kingdom.

"The personal response of the individual is all-important, Frank. Each of us must acknowledge Jesus Christ as God's Redeemer, our personal Saviour from sin, and invite Him to assume His rightful place as King of our lives; we must ask Him to enter our lives, to cleanse them, and to run them.

"Jesus has been waiting a long time to do just that, as He says in Revelation 3:20, '"Behold, I stand at the door and knock. If any man hear My voice and open the door, I will come in to him and sup with him, and he with Me."'

"The alternative, Frank, you can probably guess by now. Hebrews 9:27-28 says it: 'And as it is appointed unto men once to die, but after this the judgment; so Christ was once offered to bear the sins of many.'

"I have only this life to make the crossing to love. Beyond the grave there is no freedom to choose and no crossing. In other words, my eternal destiny depends on my choice in this life—it's Christ or continuing chaos.

"If I do nothing about Christ's offer of life, I stay on history's downward slide into eternal separation from God; but if I invite Christ into my life, I will live forever with Him. That is heaven."

Frank stares at the illustration on the envelope. He looks at Al and says, "This little illustration of yours makes more sense to me than anything I've seen. It explains some things that were completely out of focus for me."

Al smiles. "I'm glad. When I first saw it I was struck with how simple, yet profound, it is."

Frank looks at his watch. "Sorry, pal, I've got to run. But let's have lunch sometime next week and continue this further."

"Sure, any time. I'll give you a buzz."

"By the way," Frank finishes, "I'll take this envelope with me if it's OK, and look it over some more."

Any witness can adapt this illustration to his own use, of course. The two levels of human life—with and without God—become plain with this drawing and explanation.

The Chasm and the Seeker
Another illustration that has been used widely is the bridge.

Two neighbors, Joe and Pete, have known each other for several months. They borrow each other's tools, bowl together, and barbeque with their families. They get along well. Joe has been praying that the Lord would provide a way to share the Gospel with Pete, and one night Pete says out of the clear blue sky, "You know, Joe, I've never met a guy like you. You're so even-tempered. You and Marge don't fight. I've never heard you swear. Lil and I think it must have something to do with your religion. I know you go to church on Sundays and have concluded there must be something to it. But we've never been able to understand what religion is all about."

Joe can hardly believe it, but he keeps his cool and says, "Yes, we have gotten a lot of help from God. Perhaps Marge and I could come over for coffee after the kids are in bed, and we can talk. We learned a little illustration not long ago that makes it all pretty clear."

"OK. I know Lil will be interested. Come on over about 9."

That night after praying together, Joe and Marge go next door. The coffee pot is on and Pete gets to the subject. "Sit down and show us this deal. We're interested."

As the four of them sit around the table, Joe gets out a piece of paper, his Bible, and his pen, and draws this:

"Let's say this side represents man, and this side God. We're going to consider now the question: How can man and God get together? Can man bridge the gap that separates him from God and have his life in harmony with God? First let's look at some verses that reveal our present situation."

Opening his Bible to Romans 3:23, he hands it to Lil and says, "Would you read that verse?"

"Well, I'm a bit out of practice, but OK." She reads, " 'For all have sinned, and come short of the glory of God.' "

"Now, that verse says we're all in the same boat. We've all sinned. Nobody's perfect," Joe explains.

Pete nods in agreement. "OK, I'll buy that."

Joe turns the pages to Romans 6:23. He keeps the Bible this time and reads, " 'For the wages of sin is death. . . .' This verse teaches that sin earns payment. And that payment is what?"

No one answers immediately. Then Pete ventures: "Death."

"That's right. And since everyone has sinned, everyone must die. But there are two kinds of death: physical and spiritual. Our preacher told us a few Sundays ago that death in this verse means separation from God. The gap between God and man in this drawing represents the spiritual separation that you sense even while alive. The Old Testament prophet said, 'Your iniquities have separated between you and your God' (Isa. 59:2). We see then that man's sins have made a chasm between himself and God. Now let's look at another verse, Hebrews 9:27. Lil, do you want to read it, please?"

"OK. 'And as it is appointed unto men once to die, but after this the judgment.'"

"What does that passage teach, Lil?"

"I'm not very good at this, but let's see," Lil murmurs. She looks at the verse again, then hands it to Pete. "You want to try?"

The two of them think for a minute, and Pete says, "Well, one thing we know, we're all going to die someday. This verse says there's also a judgment of some kind waiting for us."

Joe nods. "Right, God will judge our sin. Here's the picture of man's total problem: we've all sinned; our sin has brought a separation from God; and when we die we face God's judgment."

Pete admits: "It's pretty clear, so far, and it doesn't sound too good, does it?"

Joe agrees. "You're right, man; it sounds terrible. But here's the good part." He turns to John 5:24 and hands it to Pete.

"'Verily, verily I say unto you, He that heareth My word, and believeth on Him that sent Me, hath everlasting life, and shall not come into condemnation, but is passed from death unto life." '"

As Pete finishes reading, Joe draws a cross over the gorge and labels it "John 5:24," with the verse's promises listed under "God."

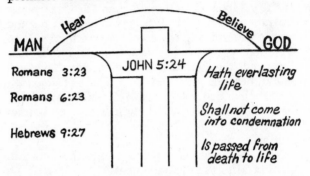

As Joe has been sharing the illustration with Pete and Lil, Marge has been quietly praying that the Holy Spirit will show them their need of the Saviour. Finally she speaks: "You know, Joe and I *heard* the Word of Christ above five years ago, and we *believed.* Our lives have never been the same. It has been so wonderful truly knowing the Lord."

Joe nods and says, "Marge has put her finger on the important thing; what we must do is hear the truth and believe. And when we do, Jesus says we will pass from one side to the other, 'from death unto life.' Not only that, He says we will also have everlasting life, and that we will not come into condemnation, that we will never face God's judgment which we talked about earlier."

"That's really something," Pete and Lil say.

"Yes," Joe agrees, "it really is. Here is another verse that makes it clearer."

He opens to John 1:12 and hands the Bible to

Lil. She reads, " 'But as many as received Him, to them gave He power to become the sons of God, even to them that believe on His name.' "

"The important truth in that verse," Joe explains, "regards what it means to believe in Christ. Here the Bible equates believing in Christ with receiving Christ. Those who have received Him into their hearts are those who truly believe in Him. Another good verse is Revelation 3:20: ' "Behold, I stand at the door and knock; if any man hear My voice and open the door, I will come in to him, and will sup with him, and he with Me." '

"The Lord Jesus Christ is saying that He stands at the door of your hearts and wants to enter your lives, give you the gift of eternal life, and forgive your sins." He looks at Pete squarely and says, "This is what we did five years ago, and it gave us something to live for. You and Lil can take the same step anytime."

Pete looks at Lil. "How about it?"

Lil is thoughtful. "Honey, I'm ready."

Joe asks them, "Do you know what to do?"

"Yes," Pete says.

Pete and Lil then pray a simple and sincere prayer and invite the Lord Jesus into their hearts. When they finish praying, Joe prays and thanks the Lord for dying for all of them on the cross to pay for their sins.

Several years ago Navigators staffer Helene Ashker met a Powers Agency model who was at the top of her field, but a loser in family life. A Christian co-worker had witnessed to her and put her in touch with Helene.

They discussed the "Bridge" together, and about half way through, the model's eyes lit up. She saw for the first time the significance of the substitutionary death of Christ, and she was ready to personally receive the One she had heard much about in the liturgy of her church.

The new Christian became an avid witness for Christ. First, she led her children to Christ; then she witnessed to co-workers. Her children are following their mother's footsteps in witnessing to their friends.

The bridge illustration has been traced to Taiwan where it was used to help Chinese refugees understand the Gospel, but doubtless it has been used around the globe at various times. It is simple and graphic, but don't expect it to accomplish your goal or to gain a decision with every use; the Holy Spirit determines this.

The Group and the Bible

Another tool that has been used increasingly in recent years is the home Bible discussion group.

Fred Wevadou of The Navigators tells what a Bible study group meant to Mark and Barb, a couple who had found everything in life but satisfaction. Mark is a graduate of the Air Force Academy and an instructor pilot for the Air Force. With all his promise in life, Mark felt an emptiness and futility in life that was typified earlier by some thoughts he recorded in his college yearbook.

"Another day gone, the sands of time hurriedly gravitating toward the unreclaimable mound of the past; grains gone but not mourned, for man eternally justifies a mundane present for the elusive future of fulfilling dreams long ago dreamt. But, alas, all too often the bright little grains of future time pass through the vortex of life's hourglass only to merge with growing discontent and illusions. . . . The tiny specks of time plummet toward their fate, and man's destiny is mirrored by the eternal hourglass: spent before fulfillment, dead without immortality, uselessly inert without the guiding hand of God."

The vehemence with which Mark and Barb assailed the hypocrisy of "social Christians" would have silenced most Christians. However, Mark had a college friend and fellow pilot named Bob, who had recently come into a new relationship with Jesus Christ. Bob did not know much Bible doctrine, but he knew what Jesus had done in his life and he desired the same for others. After months of quietly sharing his testimony, Bob convinced Mark and Barb to attend Fred's weekly Bible study for couples.

Fred relates: "We made no attempt to question their life-style and intellectual beliefs, but simply shared the Word among ourselves as they listened and questioned. Week by week their questioning became less hostile and their attitude toward the Scriptures showed they no longer felt that it was intellectual suicide to be a Christian.

"One night I noticed a marked change in their attitude toward the claims of Christ and asked them to stay afterward and talk with Bob and me. It was not long before it was clear that both of them had individually opened their hearts to Jesus earlier in the week, but had not told one another in order that their individual decisions would be genuine and uninfluenced. It's a beautiful thing to see this couple now walking together with Christ and reaching out to those around them."

Some guidelines for this kind of study are:

1. Have a supply of Bibles in the same modern-language translation to avoid fumbling for unfamiliar Scripture references. Participants can turn easily to the right page.

2. Furnish a scratch pad and pencil with each Bible for members to jot down key ideas and questions.

3. Have a leader who leads but does not dominate. Discussion should be centered in the Bible or the particular passage being studied. The conversation may jump to various life issues, but understanding is most likely when topics are restricted to the passages being discussed. Let the Lord speak to hearts from His Word, rather than any individual "proving a point."

4. The Gospel of John is a good book for study with non-Christians.*

Remember that tools are only tools, and they must be submitted to the control of the real Soul-Winner, the Spirit of God.

---

*The Navigators publishes an evangelistic Bible study tool called *A Guide for Evangelistic Bible* Studies (*using the Gospel of John*). Victor Books, Wheaton, Ill. 60187 publishes paperbacks, with leader's guides, suitable for neighborhood Bible studies.

7

WITNESSING AND WINNING

A farmer in Iowa has a number of hired hands who help with the field work, the livestock, and the maintenance of buildings and machinery. When one of his men quits, the farmer looks for a new man to help with the work in the fields.

Suppose he interviews a prospective worker who says: "Now I want you to understand from the start—I'll disc and rake and plow and plant and cultivate, but don't ask me to reap. I'll help prepare the soil and plant the seed and keep the weeds under control, but I never help bring in the crop. That's just not my line of work."

The farmer shakes his head. "Friend, you seem to have missed the point of the whole operation. The purpose of preparing the soil, planting the seed, and cultivating the growing plants is to harvest the crop."

Jesus makes a clear promise, "'And he that reapeth receiveth wages, and gathereth fruit unto life eternal, that both he that soweth and he that reapeth may rejoice together. And herein is that saying true: "One soweth, and another reapeth"; I sent you to reap that whereon you bestowed no labor; other men labored, and ye are entered into their labors'" (John 4:36-38).

These words have tremendous meaning for witnesses because Jesus said them while discussing an overripe harvest. The preceding verse gives Jesus' urgent summons that we noted earlier: "'Say not ye, there are yet four months, and then cometh harvest?' Behold, I say unto you, 'lift up your eyes, and look on the fields, for they are white already to harvest.'" Since part of God's harvest has been ripe every day and every decade since Jesus spoke these words, we should realize that one Christian sows the Gospel and another reaps the new life.

This might indicate that not every Christian is to have a ministry of reaping—or it may mean that a time lapse often separates witnessing from decision making, and Christians may participate in both. It is true that God has gifted Christians in different ways and placed us in the Body according to His will, but I believe that witnessing is more a matter of obedience than of ability. Jesus didn't say: "You clever speakers shall convince people that I am Lord and Saviour," but rather, "'You will be My witnesses . . . to the remotest end of the earth'" (Acts 1:8, BERK). We all should be witnessing, and sometimes our efforts will discover life ready to burst into bloom!

Another part of Jesus' declaration is significant to witnesses: "'I sent you to reap that whereon ye bestowed no labor.'" Someone who leads a person to Christ is usually the final link in a long chain of events. The convert has perhaps known some godly soul whose life convicted him; someone may have given him a tract or took him to church; a parent or grandparent prayed faithfully for him. The "soul-winner" is the final link—the human answer to someone's prayers. Remember that. You may have confidence, when you enter a witnessing experience, that others have already planted the Gospel seed and prayed.

As in all of life, in bringing people to Christ, we must rely completely on God. No human can "convert" a soul, but we can be used by God to contribute to this. We must remember Jesus' words: "'No man can come to Me except the Father which hath sent Me draw him'" (John 6:44). We speak in faith, trusting that the Holy Spirit will do His convicting work in the heart of the person to whom we witness.

Jesus told His disciples about the Holy Spirit's part before His own ascension to heaven. "'And when He is come, He will reprove the world of sin, and of righteousness, and of judgment: of sin, because they believe not on Me; of righteousness, because I go to My Father, and ye see Me no more; of judgment, because the prince of this world is judged'" (John 16:8-11). We do not try to do the Spirit's work, but neither can we leave to Him the work He has given us!

Consider these Scriptures prayerfully:

"If thou forbear to deliver them that are drawn unto death, and those that are ready to be slain; if thou sayest, 'Behold, we knew it not,' doth not He that pondereth the heart consider it? And He that keepeth thy soul, doth not He know it? And shall not He render to very man according to his works?" (Prov. 24:11-12)

"When I say unto the wicked, 'Thou shalt surely die'; and thou givest him not warning, nor speakest to warn the wicked from his wicked way, to save his life; the same wicked man shall die in his iniquity, but his blood will I require at thine hand. Yet if thou warn the wicked, and he turn not from his wickedness, nor from his wicked way, he shall die in his iniquity; but thou hast delivered thy soul" (Ezek. 3:18-19).

The Lord spoke to me through those solemn verses when I was a young Christian. The truths were used by God to help me set a new course for my life. I yearned to be a faithful witness, and after 25 years of sharing Christ with people, these passages still strike deep. We all have this responsibility to sow and to reap—and the great privilege of rejoicing at harvesttime!

"Will You?"

One of the simplest ways of helping a person to a decision is simply to ask: "Now that you have heard the way, will you receive Christ?"

Or, "After seeing this illustration of the Gospel, will you come to Christ now?"

Or, "Now that you know the Lord Jesus is knocking at the door of your heart, will you invite Him into your life?"

Many people answer yes at this point, and you may go through the steps we discussed earlier.

Handling a Negative Response

What should you do when a person says no? Let the conversation drift into an embarrassed silence or some new topic?

No. I usually ask, "Why?" The answer usually fits in one of three categories.

1. *"Not ready."* He needs more light—and "water" or sowing. He honestly doesn't understand enough yet and needs further time to think it through. Recommend that he read the Gospel of

John and pray before each reading that the Lord will help him sort things out. Christian bookstores have numerous excellent books that can help a non-Christian understand the Gospel. You may get one of these for him.

Pressuring a person into a decision for Christ can be devastating. A premature spiritual birth is generally a problem in life. We must not try to do what only the Lord can do. He does the drawing, making the person ready. We are to present Christ faithfully and prayerfully and give the person a clear opportunity to respond.

2. *"No good reason."* Paul ran into people like this at Athens. "And when they heard of the resurrection of the dead, some mocked; and others said, 'We will hear thee again of this matter.' So Paul departed from among them. Howbeit certain men clave unto him, and believed; among which was Dionysius, the Areopagite, and a woman named Damaris, and others with them" (Acts 17:32-34).

Often we will talk with people who agree that the Gospel sounds appealing. They admire your sincerity, but they are not going to do anything about it now. These people are in a dangerous position, and I tell them so. Each of us may be just one heartbeat from eternity, and the unsaved person must understand this. In such situations, I may point out these Scriptures:

" 'Come *now*, and let us reason together,' saith the Lord; 'though your sins be as scarlet, they shall be as white as snow; though they be red like crimson, they shall be as wool' " (Isa. 1:18).

"Remember *now* thy Creator in the days of thy youth, while the evil days come not, nor the years draw nigh, when thou shalt say, 'I have no pleasure in them' " (Eccl. 12:1).

"Boast not thyself of tomorrow, for thou knowest not what a day may bring forth" (Prov. 27:1).

"He that being often reproved hardeneth his neck, shall suddenly be destroyed, and that without remedy" (Prov. 29:1).

"Behold, *now* is the accepted time; behold, *now* is the day of salvation" (2 Cor. 6:2).

"Choose you *this day* whom ye will serve" (Josh. 24:15).

Once while sharing the Gospel with a young American in Germany, I noticed he had a cocky attitude. He kept listening, so I continued to present Christ. When I finished, I asked if he would like to receive the Lord Jesus into his life. He said no, so I asked why. He said he knew it was all true, he should take the step, but he was not going to do it.

I've never done this before or since, but there was something in his attitude toward God that made me fear for his future. I suggested we have a short prayer before we parted and that he tell the Lord he knew Jesus died on the cross for his sins and was standing at the door of his heart, but he was turning Him away. I told him to tell Jesus he knew of His love for him, but he was rejecting the Saviour and asking Him to go away.

The guy looked a bit shocked, but I bowed my head and waited. After several moments he reached over and tapped me on the shoulder and said, "I can't say that."

I looked at him and replied, "But that's what you *are* saying—only you're telling it to me instead of Him." He was subdued by the thought, but went away uncommitted. However, later that night he asked Christ into his life.

3. *Genuine obstacles.* The third category includes honest hang-ups or problems. Let me list a few:

- *"I'm afraid I can't hold out."*

A friend came to our home for an evening meal. After dinner, he remarked about our prayer of thanksgiving at the table, and I easily widened the topic to spiritual matters. After sharing the way to Christ, I asked if he would like to become a follower of Christ. He said, "Lee, I'm afraid I couldn't hold out. I've got something in my life that runs pretty deep, and I'm afraid that after I made a decision like you talked about, I'd soon go back to the old ways."

I told him that I understood his problem. Many people have a struggle with sin after they make their decision for the Lord. But there is help for this problem in the Scriptures.

I quoted 1 Corinthians 10:13, "There hath no temptation taken you but such as is common to man. But God is faithful, who will not suffer you to be tempted above that ye are able, but will with the temptation also make a way to escape, that ye may be able to bear it."

This verse assures us that when the devil tempts us to sin, the Lord faithfully provides a way out. And He keeps the temptations from being more than we can handle if we call on His strength.

Another powerful fact is that Christians become "partakers of the divine nature," drawing on superhuman character. Peter says, "Whereby are given unto us exceeding great and precious promises, that by these ye might be partakers of the divine nature, having escaped the corruption that is in the world through lust" (2 Peter 1:4). And, of course, Christ makes us a new person when we receive Him, for "if any man be in Christ, he is a new creature; old things are passed away; behold, all things are become new" (2 Cor. 5:17).

I gave the young man the illustration of the caterpillar. It craws along in the dirt as a worm, bound to the earth. Then one day it enters a cocoon. Over a period of time, a metamorphosis takes place, and eventually it emerges a butterfly, a brand new creature. No longer does it crawl in the dirt; it is a creature made for a different kind of life, enjoying a higher plane. As a "partaker of the divine nature" to whom "old things are passed away" and "all things are become new," the Christian is fully prepared to conquer old habits and allurements.

• *"I'm afraid I've gone too far; God could never forgive me."*

I talked to a young Communist in Europe who was ridden with guilt. He had deeply offended his mother, and the memory hung like a lead weight on him. I had the joy of explaining the Gospel to him, but he couldn't imagine that God, if He existed, could forgive such a grievous act as his.

Saul, who became Paul after his conversion to Christ, was at least indirectly a murderer. In his misguided zeal for God, he was "breathing out threatenings and slaughter against the disciples of the Lord" (Acts 9:1). When Stephen was stoned to death, Saul stood near, "consenting unto his death" (Acts 8:1). Yet God forgave Saul. God not only forgave him, but used him mightily as the apostle to the Gentiles and the writer of much of our New Testament.

Our sin can never exceed the grace of God. The Scriptures are full of this astonishing truth. When we come to Christ, no matter what our past, we are clothed in His righteousness. We see this both in the Old Testament ("For He hath clothed me . . . with the robe of righteousness"—Isa. 61:10), and in the New ("And be found in Him, not having

mine own righteousness, which is of the law, but
that which is through the faith of Christ, the righteousness which is of God by faith"—Phil. 3:9).

• *"I'm as good as the next guy. I'll take my
chances."*

This fellow is at the opposite end of the spectrum
from the previous one. His problem is, he just
doesn't understand the sin problem. My answer to
him is, "Yes, you're as good as the next guy, but
have you taken a close look at the next guy?"

The Bible clearly indicates that the next guy has
the same problem—and it's big. "For all have
sinned, and come short of the glory of God" (Rom.
3:23) indicates that every human is guilty before
God and is subject to judgment. There are no
"little sins" in God's view.

The Bible also describes sin as going astray. "All
we like sheep have gone astray" (Isa. 53:6). We
are like an archer trying to hit a bulls-eye and his
arrows fall short of the mark. The person who
compares his virtue with others is lining up one
failure beside other failures and taking comfort in
the company of losers! The only safe comparison is
with Jesus Christ, "who did no sin, neither was
guile found in His mouth" (1 Peter 2:22). This is
the standard we must match—or beg God's forgiveness and cleansing!

• *"I see too many hypocrites in the church today."*

Yes, there are hypocrites in the church, and
that fact demonstrates there is also the genuine
product, the truly new person whom the hypocrite
tries to counterfeit!

A city slicker reportedly traveled into the hills
and stopped at a country store. He asked the
salesboy, "Will you change this $13 bill for me?"

The salesboy called to his dad out back, "There's a feller here who wants change for a $13 bill. Shall we give it to him?"

His dad called back, "Sure, Son; give him two threes and a seven."

The cheap imitation always trails the path of the valued original, and the presence of hypocrites in the church confirms the reality of lives changed by Christ.

• *"The whole thing is a hoax."*

A group of young atheists told me one time that I was "Utopian—living in a dream world. What you're saying about a new life is frankly just too good to be true."

A college student in Idaho made a similar remark. A girl heard this comment and came to my defense. "No, it's not a dream," she said. "It happened to me last year." Then she gave her testimony. The guy listened and was silenced by the authenticity of her personal experiences.

Your testimony is the best answer for such a remark. It is not theory, nor philosophy, but factual history! At a point of time in a real world, you lived it. Just tell what happened to you, as Psalm 107:2 urges: "Let the redeemed of the Lord say so, whom He hath redeemed from the hand of the enemy."

The solution for this doubter's problem is to try an experiment. Asking Christ into his life will show him if Jesus' offer is real. Challenge the skeptic to be intellectually honest and to make the trial. We can be confident of the result, just as David was: "O taste and see that the Lord is good; blessed is the man that trusteth in Him" (Ps. 34:8).

• *"What will my friends think?"*

Many inquirers are intimidated by the reaction

friends may show. They are afraid of losing their respect or friendship.

I was witnessing to a young man at a Midwestern university who listened intently to the Gospel. He lived in a fraternity on campus and was a popular student. When I asked him if he would like to receive Christ, he thought for a moment and then said, "What will the guys say if I take this step?"

"What guys?" I asked.

"Oh, the guys in the house."

"Well," I said, "let's make a list of the guys in this house who would object to your becoming a Christian." We ended up with the names of six guys. It turned out that all of them were heavy drinkers and poor students. I asked, "Would you rather have your life governed by God or by these six drunks? That's what the picture is. You are either going to bow to the will of God or bow to the will of these six drunks. Which will it be?"

He chose Christ.

People must realize that they have to stand before God one day and give account of their lives. Each person will be alone, with no friends to hide behind or hold them up. What God says and thinks is far more important than the opinion of friends. God's decision will be: "And whosoever was not found written in the book of life was cast into the lake of fire" (Rev. 20:15).

• *"I want to enjoy life."*

The way of the world appears exciting, satisfying, and attractive—until a person plunges in and discovers its mirages, dead-ends and heartless travelers.

Many people have told me how they broke the apron strings of home life and headed off to college or military service with high expectations for a wonderful life. They "lived it up," trifling with one sin, then another. The deeper they got involved in the things of "the world, the flesh, and the devil," the more they ached with emptiness. Life was tasteless and drab.

A distorted view of God causes this twisted view of the "good life." Many think of God as sort of an overhanging glacier which drops on wrongdoers, or as some kind of cosmic policeman only interested in preventing human beings from having any fun in life.

The fact is that Christ came to give us the abundant life, not to take it from us. He brought joy, not gloom. He instills meaning and purpose, not frustration. He said, "'I am come that they might have life, and that they might have it more abundantly'" (John 10:10), and He accomplished this goal as He did every other objective.

• *"I grew up in the church."*

Many people say, "I think I believe. I used to go to Sunday School and church all the time when I was a kid, and I've even prayed some. I've been baptized; I've joined the church."

These people do understand something about the Bible and the things of God, but many of them have "churchianity," not Christianity. The tragedy is that they are missing the kingdom of God by about 18 inches—the distance between their heads and their hearts. Romans 10:9-10 points out, "If thou shalt confess with thy mouth the Lord Jesus, and shalt believe in thine heart that God hath raised Him from the dead, thou shalt be saved. For with the heart man believeth unto righteousness, and with the mouth confession is made unto salvation." Many people know enough about Christ to be saved, but they haven't taken the step of commitment. With the heart—or will—a person believes and receives Christ's righteousness.

One reply for this person is, "I realize that you have done all these things, but have you ever personally received Christ?"

If there is any doubt, a person should make sure of his position. John 1:12 says that "as many as *received Him*, to them gave He power to become the sons of God." It is not, "as many as went to church," or "as many as taught Sunday School." Only *those who received Him* were given power to become sons of God.

They Don't Know How

I am convinced that the reason multitudes of people in the United States have not yet received Christ—though they are ready—is that they do not know how. First, they do not know that a personal decision for Christ is necessary. Second, they do not know Christ is standing at the door of their hearts, waiting to come in. And they do not know that He will enter their lives if they will pray and invite Him in to be their personal Saviour and Lord.

An unusual experience convinced me of this. I was sharing the Gospel with a young man. When I finished, I asked, "Now that you've heard the message of the Gospel, what is your reaction? Will you receive Christ?"

Immediately he said, "Yes."

A little surprised, I asked him, "How long have you been thinking about making this decision for Christ?"

"Three years," he said.

"Why didn't you do it before this?"

"No one ever showed me how."

"Do you mean to tell me that you have wanted

to come to Christ but you didn't know how, and that's what has kept you from it?"

"Yes," he told me.

I explained in very simple terms how to receive Christ, and he did so on the spot.

An hour later I was sharing Christ with another young man. When I finished, I asked if he would like to receive Christ, and he said yes. I asked him also, "How long have you been thinking about making this decision for Christ?"

"Three months."

"Why didn't you do it before this?"

"I didn't know how."

An hour later I was sharing the Gospel with a third young man. When I finished the presentation I asked him, "Would you like to receive Christ now?" His reply was the same.

"How long have you been thinking about making this decision for Christ?"

"Three days."

"Why didn't you do it three days ago?"

"Well, I was in church last Sunday and the preacher talked about our need for Christ, and I became convinced that I needed Him, but I didn't know what to do. Fortunately," he continued, "you've come along and explained it to me."

He then received Christ.

Gospel planters have sowed great stretches of America, and the harvest is waiting for reapers who know how believers are born.

One thing witnesses should never neglect is to make clear that receiving Christ is responding to a *living option*—a choice that has momentous consequences.

I live on a fairly quiet street, so when I leave my car at the curb at night it is likely to be safe.

However, if I stall my car on a railroad crossing and leave it very long, I risk losing my means of transportation.

Thus it is with our decision for Christ: receiving or rejecting Christ determines our gain or loss for eternity. "He that believeth on the Son hath everlasting life; and he that believeth not the Son shall not see life, but the wrath of God abideth on him" (John 3:36).

Do what you can to help a person make his decision for Christ, but if he is not ready, do not try to win a soul that needs additional witness. You may be the final link in a chain that connects a person to Christ—or you may be one of the essential earlier links that help complete the eventual union.

8

IT'S ALIVE!

I can still hear the warning from some older Christians when I started witnessing: "Don't club people over the head with the Bible. They will think you are a religious nut. Keep your Bible out of sight or you'll scare people away. Remember, Proverbs 1:17 says, 'Surely in vain the net is spread in the sight of any bird.'"

Twenty-five years ago the Bible did "turn off" many non-Christian Americans. Possibly this was caused more by "Bible-thumpers" than by reaction against the Bible itself. Most non-Christians know little about the Bible, and I think they have always been surprised to learn things it actually says.

Unlike other books, the Bible uniquely is *alive* and *powerful*.

The Prophet Jeremiah draws an interesting analogy in comparing man's word with the Word of God. "'The prophet that hath a dream, let him tell a dream; and he that hath My Word, let him speak My Word faithfully. What is the chaff to the wheat?' saith the Lord" (Jer. 23:28). God likens man's word to chaff and His to wheat.

If a farmer were to plant a wagonload of chaff, what would he reap? Nothing! There is no life in the chaff. But if he plants a bushel of wheat, he will reap a crop of wheat. There is life in wheat seed, life that germinates and multiplies.

In Jesus' illustration of the farmer-witness, He said, "The sower soweth the *Word.*" God's Word is the seed by which we are born again. This is confirmed in 1 Peter 1:23: "Being born again, not of corruptible seed, but of incorruptible, by the Word of God, which liveth and abideth for ever."

Sam Meets the Word

Some years ago I met a man named Sam at a Christian conference outside of Washington, D.C. He was a new Christian and as we ate together he gave his testimony.

As a young instructor in a Pennsylvania college, he admitted to a perverse hobby: making Christians look like fools. He taught math and philosophy and was popular with students. Being a weight-lifter, handsome, and the owner of a shiny convertible gave him an enviable image on campus.

One day a friend of mine named Gene Tabor was on campus witnessing to one of the students. The student asked, "Have you ever talked to Sam?"

"Sam who?"

"Come on, I'll introduce you."

So Gene and the student looked up Sam, who preceeded to do his thing. Gene listened carefully a while, then asked, "Sam, has anyone ever shared with you just what the good news of the Gospel really is?"

"No, I don't think so," he replied.

"Well, would you mind if I took a few minutes and shared it?"

"OK. Go ahead."

Gene opened his Bible and very simply shared verse after verse with Sam, explaining the message in clear terms. When Gene finished, he shook hands with Sam and thanked him for his time. No argument. Gene went back to his home in Washington, D.C. and enlisted prayer for Sam.

Some weeks later Sam was in his room going over student papers when suddenly, as he put it, "A great wave of depression came over me. I sensed a tremendous lostness, a terrible feeling of being cut off from God. I fell headlong on my bed and cried out to God for mercy, and after about an hour I knew that He had answered. Christ had saved me."

The next day, Sunday, Sam decided to go to Sunday School and church. He didn't find a church that preached the Word of God and salvation through Jesus Christ, so he drove up into the mountains, looking for a church that would instruct him in his newfound faith.

In a small town he spotted a church and went to the men's Bible class. The teacher was an older man, and Sam thought he must know God and be a wise teacher. The teacher asked Sam his name and where he lived. Sam introduced himself, then related how he had become a believer in Christ the day before.

Sam was in for a surprise. The teacher took issue with Sam about his faith in Christ and spent much of the class session deriding the idea of "coming to Christ," and "being born again." When Sam left the class he thought to himself, "I don't know much, but I know more than he does!"

Shortly after that, Sam found a Bible-teaching church and began to grow. He heard about a Christian conference, went to it, and that's where I met him and heard his story.

When he finished his testimony, I asked if he had witnessed to any of his fellow instructors. He said no, but he thought it would be a good idea. I asked if he would like for me to come to the campus, and we could talk together to a few of his friends. He eagerly agreed.

I planned with three other Christians to make the visit, but on the scheduled day I had to go instead to Norfolk, Va. The other three went without me. When they arrived on campus, they went to the student union and were met by a young man who spotted their Bibles and asked if they had come to see Sam. They said yes. He directed them downstairs. There they found the largest room in the student union full to overflowing and the corridor jammed with students besides. Sam had advertised all over campus that men were coming to answer questions about God and the Bible, and this was the turnout.

In the meeting a student asked, "What is it like to come to Jesus?" Jim White, one of the members of the three-man team, suggested that Sam tell the students his personal experience.

You can imagine the effect that had on the assembled students. Brilliant, handsome, popular Sam, whose hobby had been making fools out of Christians, was telling his admirers how to join the winners.

As I reflected on Sam's story, I considered various things that had *not* made him a new person. It wasn't someone's power of persuasion. No dynamic extrovert had bowled him over with a charming personality and catch phrases. He hadn't succumbed to superior philosophical arguments. No, a

Christian who loved Christ and knew the Good
News had quietly shared the Word of God with
Sam and enlisted Christians to pray for him—and
the Holy Spirit did His convicting work. God's
planted seed erupted into life!

The Word's Creative Power

The Gospel of Jesus Christ is persuasive but it is
more: it is *creative*. It creates new life. As witnesses, we don't need debating talent or a plan
to win an argument; we need to share God's Word
faithfully, pray, and trust the Holy Spirit to bring
forth life.

It is hard for us to imagine how powerful the
Word of God is. Hebrews 4:12 describes it this
way: "For the Word of God is quick, and powerful,
and sharper than any two-edged sword, piercing
even to the dividing asunder of soul and spirit, and
of the joints and marrow, and is a discerner of the
thoughts and intents of the heart." Can you conceive of a sharper spiritual scalpel?

Another description is recorded by Jeremiah:
"'Is not My Word like as a fire?' saith the Lord;
'and like a hammer that breaketh the rock in
pieces?'" (23:29)

A number of years ago my wife, Virginia, was
helping a new Christian take her early steps with
the Lord. The new Christian asked if someone
would talk to her father about Christ. I accepted
her invitation, though I was a fairly new Christian
myself.

When I arrived at the man's house I was stunned
to learn that he could not speak or read English!
He was a big, ramrod-straight Russian with a
handlebar mustache and steel-gray eyes that bored
through me. In addition, he was not at all happy

with my visit. He told his daughter Erika to have me sit down, and I was very grateful for that because my wobbly knees were about to collapse under me!

Somehow I remembered to send up a quick prayer to the Lord for help. Then the idea hit me to ask if there was a Russian Bible in the house. There was.

"Will your dad read it?" I asked Erika.

"He says he will."

Erika then brought out a large Russian Bible, and he took it in his huge hands and sat looking at me. Through Erika, I had him look up specific verses, and he would read them out loud. We started with verses about his separation from God because of sin, then found passages about God's love for him, followed by verses explaining the saving power of Christ's death on the cross. We read many verses that made the message clear. I silently thanked God during our progress that a young man had helped me as a brand new Christian to get started in memorizing Scripture so I didn't have to search for it!

After what seemed an eternity I noticed a change of attitude, a different look in the man's eyes. I began to have him read invitation verses: "'All that the Father giveth Me shall come to Me; and him that cometh to Me I will in no wise cast out'" (John 6:37). "'Come unto Me, all ye that labor and are heavy laden, and I will give you rest. Take My yoke upon you, and learn of Me; for I am meek and lowly in heart; and ye shall find rest unto your souls'" (Matt. 11:28-29).

Suddenly the huge man's shoulders slumped; he bowed his head and began to cry—deep sobs like you hear at a funeral. And he began to pray aloud.

I couldn't understand a word but I recognized the prayer; I had prayed it myself three years earlier. Another sinner had come to the foot of the cross.

I could not say one word to the man directly, but God did. That's what counts. God used His Word to bring another eternal soul to Himself.

A Killer Meets the Word

I once read a story about a bandit chief in India. He killed and robbed his victims on the deserted roads of his territory. One day he noticed a small, black book on a man he had just killed. This book's pages were especially thin—just right for rolling cigarettes, he thought. He took the book and tore out a page when he needed a smoke. Soon he noticed the book was written in his language and he began reading. In this small New Testament, he discovered the message of God's love for him and the offer of eternal life through faith in Christ. The Holy Spirit used His Book to draw the man to faith and repentance. Shortly after his conversion, the murderer went to his village and surrendered himself to officials. In prison he became an ardent witness for Christ.

Gypsies Meet the Word

While traveling in Scandinavia, I was asked by a pastor if I knew of any strong evangelical work in a certain sector of Eastern Europe. I didn't, and he began to tell me this story.

A band of gypsies set up camp outside a certain village and surreptitiously took things from houses in the town. One of the things they stole was a black book. In the evenings the camp gathered around the fire and one of the young men read from the black book. According to the pastor, the entire camp repented of their sins, professed Christ, and returned the stolen articles. The chronic thieves were made honest by the Book and its divine Author.

The Cannibal Meets the Word

Sometime ago I read about a South Sea island trader who braved the Pacific Ocean during the days of the great sailing vessels.

When landing on one of the islands, he noticed a handsome, muscular youth lounging against a palm tree reading a large, black book. Approaching the young man, he saw it was a Bible. The visitor smiled and said, "Young man, I don't want to discourage your study of that Book, but you should know that where I'm from it is very much out of fashion."

The young man smiled broadly and replied, "Sir, if this Book were out of fashion here, I would kill and eat you!"

And he wasn't joking. He had been made new by a Book that is "living and powerful."

Exciting! And yet many of God's people do not know God's Word well enough to loose its power!

I vividly recall an incident in the South Pacific where I was serving with the Marines in World War II. During an invasion we rolled up the beach and an enemy shell crashed through our amphibious tank, landing in a pile of our .75 caliber shells. Miraculously the ammunition didn't blow up, and we left that tank in a hurry! I moved from tree to tree, bush to bush, hole to hole, cautiously working my way inland. The sergeant came up beside me and said, "You OK?"

"Yup."

"Where's your helmet?"

I felt my head. "Must be back in the tank, Sarge," I answered.

"Where's your duty belt?"

On our duty belt we carried our canteens, knife, and so on. "Must be back in the tank, Sarge," I muttered. Then, with an irate shout the sergeant prodded: "As a matter of fact, Eims, where's your *rifle?*" My rifle was also back in the tank—I was making my way toward the enemy totally une-quipped for battle!

That's the way it is with many Christians today. To be ready for spiritual victories, we must spend time in the Word of God: study it, memorize it, meditate on it so we can communicate it. Remember, spiritually dead people are born again, "not of corruptible seed but of incorruptible, by the Word of God which liveth and abideth forever," and His Word is "living and powerful and sharper than any two-edged sword."

9

PRAYER POWER

The voice on the phone was tense and projected a sense of urgency. "Is this Mr. Eims?"

I told her it was.

"Do you know a girl named Anita in nurses training in Kansas City?"

"I sure do."

"Well, Mr. Eims, Anita often talked about you and now I've got a favor to ask. I was in training with her and she talked to me about my need for Jesus. I'm not interested in that sort of thing and told her so. In fact, I made fun of her. Just before we graduated she told me she was going to pray that I would have no peace in my soul until I came to Jesus. I laughed at her, but the awful thing is, I haven't had a good night's sleep since she began praying. Now here's the favor: I want you to pray and cancel out her prayers!"

I explained to the girl that there was no way I could do that. Anita had a direct line to God and there was no way I could tap it.

"That's not fair!" she exploded. "Surely there's something you can do about her prayers." She continued to talk and plead. In fact, she kept me on the phone for over two hours. Finally she hung up in frustration.

The next day, having just returned from Sunday School and church, our family was sitting down to the Sunday meal. The phone rang, and the same girl with a new voice said, "I just had to tell you that it's all over. Last night I couldn't take it any longer so I got out of bed and did what I knew I should have done all along. I invited Jesus into my heart about 2:30 A.M. I'm not sure how to explain this but it was like a big load rolled off my back." I assured her I knew just what she meant; I had one roll off my back a few years ago when I came to Jesus.

"Well, anyway, I just wanted to call you and tell you what I've done," she said. "And by the way, I slept great last night after I prayed to Jesus."

Quite a few years have passed since I talked with that girl, and over the years the Lord has reinforced the conviction that prayer is a vital force in witnessing.

Four Power Points of Prayer

Prayer is vital in witnessing in at least four ways.

1. *Prayer prepares a heart to receive Christ.* I was trying to explain this truth to one of my children when I noticed the bright Colorado sun beaming through our window. I asked my son what would happen if we put a lump of clay on the window sill. He said it would get hard. I then asked what would happen if we put a piece of chocolate there. He said it would melt. I asked him why the difference. He thought a minute and said, "Because they are made of different stuff."

So it is with the human heart. We've seen the

light of the Gospel of Christ shine on a heart and make it hard with resistance. Others hearts melt under the warm light, and respond joyfully to the message of salvation. In some cases, this contrasting result may indicate that the heart of the one person was not prepared by the prayers of Christians while the other was.

2. *Prayer opens opportunities to witness.* Paul asked the Colossians to pray for his ministry. "Continue in prayer . . . that God would open into us a door of utterance, to speak the mystery of Christ, for which I am also in bonds; that I may make it manifest, as I ought to speak" (Col. 4:2-4).

A strange truth shines from this passage. Though Paul was confident of God's commission to go and witness, he believed it was vital that Christians ask God for open doors for him. The pray-ers were sharing in the witnessing.

A fellow named Bill Cole lived with us for a while. Once when my wife and I were going away for the day, leaving Bill to fix a gate in the back yard and trim some bushes, he and I committed the day's activities to the Lord in prayer. I noticed that Bill didn't pray about his work for the day, but for an opportunity to witness. I must admit that his request annoyed me. *Why is he praying about that?* I thought. *Why doesn't he pray that he will do a good job on the day's tasks?*

As Virginia and I left, however, Bill was on the front porch talking to the milkman about the Lord. The milkman appeared keenly interested. We were away for about an hour when we had to return to pick up something. This time Bill was talking to the meterman—about the Lord, naturally!

I learned that day if you want to witness, pray!

3. *Specific prayers bring specific answers.* The third thing to remember about prayer and witnessing is to be very specific. Pray for people by name. Jesus said, "'And whatsoever ye shall ask in My name, that will I do, that the Father may be glorified in the Son. If ye shall ask anything in My name, I will do it'" (John 14:13-14).

During the island-hopping advance across the Pacific in World War II, the marines usually landed after offshore navy guns pounded island defenses for days. But when we marines went ashore and began fighting our way inland, we found that the bombardment by the big guns had done very little damage. The enemy had a network of caves deep within the high ranges of the islands, and the defenders went underground when the shooting started. I doubt if our guns had even kept them awake.

Once we got within rifle range, good marksmanship began to count. A marine would be wounded and a corpsman would go out to tend to him. Then he too would be shot. Another corpsman would go to their rescue, and he would be picked off. A sniper out there was eliminating our medical team! One man with a rifle was doing more damage to us than our entire fleet had done to them in five days of heavy shelling.

Specific prayer has potent accuracy. We can pray general prayers for "the lost"; we can pray for "the heathen in darkest Africa." But we must beware lest we get caught up in praying for the lost millions and forget to pray for lost Bill Jones. For specific answers, pray for people by name.

4. *Persistent prayer is rewarded.* The fourth thing for witnesses to remember about prayer is never to give up! Unless we follow Jesus' admonition in

Luke 18:1 that "men ought always to pray, and not to faint," we may lose heart—and much blessing—before God saves those for whom we are praying.

When I became a Christian, I was zealous to win others but I had little tact. I made some of my worst mistakes with my parents. I would send them letters saying they were sinners on the road to hell, and quote Scripture verses that told of the rich man who died and went to hell. I meant well, but I was not considerate of their feelings and past experience.

After some time a mature Christian convinced me that the most effective thing to do regarding my parents' salvation was to pray for them.

I began praying, and God worked first in my mother's heart. She had believed that good deeds and an upright life were the way to heaven. One day I came across these words in the Bible: "Then said they unto Him, 'What shall we do, that we might work the works of God?' Jesus answered, and said unto them, 'This is the work of God, that ye believe on Him whom He hath sent'" (John 6:28-29).

I let out a yelp of excitement and ran into the room where my mother was. "Mom!" I said, "Look at this!" She read it, and shortly after that she placed her complete trust in the Saviour. That verse helped her to see that salvation was not by good works but by faith.

Later, at a prayer meeting in our small church in Council Bluffs, Iowa, I requested prayer that my dad would come to Christ as well. When the meeting was over, an elderly gentleman came to me and suggested that in addition to praying for my dad perhaps he should talk to him. I was elated and told him I hoped he would.

About a week later this man and a friend drove the 20 miles to my dad's house. Dad was outraged and demanded they leave his house. He was tough on the outside and rock-hard on the inside.

I knew nothing about this at the time and continued to pray. I had prayed for him every day for seven years, though there seemed to be no sign of a response. About a month after their first visit, the same men paid Dad the second call. As soon as Dad saw them, he invited them into the house, started weeping, and walked over to the davenport where he knelt down and began to pray! That evening he received Christ into his heart.

Shortly afterward I got a long letter from the elderly visitor describing what had happened. I was so happy I could hardly stand it.

Six months later my dad was dead—to us, but living in heaven!

When Jesus says that men should always pray and not lose hope, I believe Him! Jesus wants us to win by praying as well as by witnessing.

If you want to see particular persons won to Christ, I suggest you put their names on a prayer list. Then pray for opportunities to share the Gospel with them, ask God to prepare their hearts, and pray until God gives the promised answer!

Prayer is a powerful force. Remember Jesus' words spoken shortly before He left His followers to return to His Father: "'Hitherto have ye asked nothing in My name; ask, and ye shall receive, that your joy may be full'" (John 16:24).

10

THE
INDISPENSABLE LINK

When I was a new Christian, Dawson Trotman, founder of The Navigators, gave me some of the best advice I've ever received. He said, "Don't get so involved in the work of the kingdom that you don't have time to spend with the King."

Another friend of mine, Russ Johnston, put it this way: "Unless your intake exceeds your output, the upkeep will be your downfall."

How true! Yet I meet Christians all the time who are too busy to attend to the most important part of their lives. They are in this club, that circle, a couple of committees, running about in circles, out of breath, honking at their own tail-lights in a busy swirl of activity.

If you're in this fix, I advise you to slow down. Your good can be the enemy of the best.

Stunted Relationship

Remember the story of Mary and Martha? (See Luke 10:38-42). Martha was anxious and troubled about *many* things, but Jesus reminded her, *"One thing is needful."*

What thing?

Fellowship with Jesus.

A young man I knew in the service spent hours of his free time studying the Word of God and praying. He memorized hundreds of passages of Scripture, and his life was very fruitful for God. When he was discharged and went home, his church was amazed at his spiritual growth while in the military. They immediately put him to work heading up a young people's project, sponsoring a new group, and planning picnics and parties for idle kids. He became so busy that Bible study and prayer were crowded out of his schedule. His Scripture memorizing lapsed, and he forgot most of the verses he had learned. He got so involved in the work of the kingdom that he missed the signals of the King.

Jesus has some powerful words for us: " 'Abide in Me, and I in you. As the branch cannot bear fruit of itself, except it abide in the vine; no more can ye, except ye abide in Me. I am the Vine, ye are the branches; he that abideth in Me, and I in him, the same bringeth forth much fruit; for without Me ye can do nothing' " (John 15:4-5).

Did you notice the word "nothing"? Jesus is saying the purpose of a vine is to bear fruit; and unless we live in vital, daily fellowship with Him, we will not bear fruit. This is so because, though the fruit appears on the branch, the *source* of fruit-fulness is the vine. Being fruitful is not an activity but a way of life—fruitfulness is a result of fellowship with Christ.

Salvation did not originate with man, and it cannot be propagated by humans. It is not like a Red Cross drive that can be organized and carried out through planning and hard work.

It is *God* who is "not willing that any should perish" (2 Peter 3:9).

It is *God* "who will have all men to be saved" (1 Tim. 2:4).

It is *God* who "so loved the world, that He gave His only begotten Son" (John 3:16).

It is *God* who sent His Son "to seek and to save that which was lost" (Luke 19:10).

It is *God* who "added to the Church" (Acts 2:47).

"It is *God* that worketh in you both to will and to do of His good pleasure" (Phil. 2:13).

It is God, not man. God's agency, not human energy.

Remember these words of Jesus: " 'Follow Me, and I will make you fishers of men' " (Matt. 4:19). Follow—live in vital union and fellowship with Jesus—in order to see life reproduced. As Jesus reproved the toiling Martha, He tells us: *"One thing* is needful."

So the foremost concern of Christians desiring to serve Christ must be a strong relationship with Him. Anything less than a strong vertical relationship jeopardizes the spiritual vitality of horizontal relationships. The effectiveness of our witness stands or falls according to our personal fellowship with Christ. Man cannot do God's work, but he can be used by God to do it.

Paul's statement to the Romans illustrates this important truth: "For I will not dare to speak of any of those things which Christ hath not wrought by me, to make the Gentiles obedient, by word and deed" (Rom. 15:18).

Notice who is said to be working in the lives of the Gentiles: Christ.

And how is Christ teaching them? By Paul.

Jesus was doing the work in human lives, but He

was using Paul as an instrument. A right-angled triangle depicts this relationship.

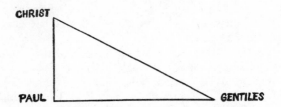

As the drawing shows, Paul, the Christian, communicated with Christ and then communicated the Gospel to his fellow men. The upward communion is essential for the horizontal connection.

The Source of Life

Gentleman farmer Augustus Brown started an apple orchard. When it did not produce fruit, he became upset. He began to think of ways to correct the problem.

First, he hired the high school band to march up and down the road in front of the orchard and play stirring music. Batons twirled, and cheer leaders yelled, while Farmer Brown jumped up and down and shouted: "Come on, trees; I know you can do it."

The trees only shook their leaves in bewilderment.

Farmer Brown knew other orchards produced fruit, so he tried another approach. He hired a noted violinist to visit the orchard and play a soulful, introspective tune while he coaxed the trees to yield apples. He wept; he bared his soul, expressing his concern for their condition: "It's not me I'm thinking about, but you. I long to see you fulfill your destiny. Apples, come forth!"

The dead stillness that followed was more suited to a cemetery than a healthy orchard.

The distraught farmer decided he was being too soft on the worthless trees. Manual in hand, he marched out to the orchard and began to read the riot act. He pointed out their ugliness. He raved about their flaws. He reminded them of the flourishing orchards around them. "Look at Farmer Green's trees," he railed. "And look at Farmer White's and Farmer Black's trees." He was merciless and unequivocal. He pounded on his "orchard manual" with authority and looked up into the sky as if to call down lightning. But no apples appeared.

Defeated, he stared at the big black manual with tear-dimmed eyes and glimpsed some arresting words. He began reading to himself and became excited. The message was full of good ideas.

The next morning he brought fertilizer and water and began tending the trees. He pruned them, dug around their roots, and watered them well. Very soon the trees blossomed, and in due time Farmer Brown had apples! He had linked up with life.

God often likens men to trees in the Scriptures. "And he shall be like a tree planted by the rivers of water, that bringeth forth his fruit in his season, his leaf also shall not wither; and whatsoever he doeth shall prosper" (Ps. 1:3).

"Blessed is the man that trusteth in the Lord, and whose hope the Lord is. For he shall be as a tree planted by the waters, and that spreadeth out her roots by the river, and shall not see when heat cometh, but her leaf shall be green; and shall not be careful in the year of drought neither shall cease from yielding fruit" (Jer. 17:7-8).

As men are likened to trees, the Word of God is likened to water.

" 'For as the rain cometh down, and the snow from heaven, and returneth not thither, but watereth the earth, and maketh it bring forth and bud, that it may give seed to the sower, and bread to the eater; so shall My Word be that goeth forth out of My mouth: it shall not return unto Me void, but it shall accomplish that which I please, and it shall prosper in the thing whereto I sent it' " (Isa. 55:10-11).

"Christ also loved the Church, and gave Himself for it; that He might sanctify and cleanse it with the washing of water by the Word" (Eph. 5:25-26).

The Fellowship of the Word

A fruitful Christian must get his spiritual roots deep into the life-giving wells of the Word of God. This refreshing supply courses from the Lord Jesus Christ. He said He is the Water of life, and His fountain renews life as well as begins it.

Our great enemy, Satan, thrives in the arid places of experience. He tempted Jesus in the parched wilderness, and he likes to waylay Christians today who are weakened by a drought of fellowship with the Lord. Our safeguard is Jesus' life, flowing through His Word.

How can we prosper more from the Word?

1. *We can go where it is faithfully taught.* One of the piercing questions asked by Jesus was, "When the Son of Man cometh, shall He find faith on the earth?" (Luke 18:8) Should He come today, how much faith would He find in you?

"We walk by faith," Paul said, "not by sight" (2 Cor. 5:7). How straight and strong and serene are you walking?

This indispensable faith is a gift from God, we learn in Ephesians 2:8. God has also appointed a definite means for communicating this gift: "Faith cometh by hearing, and hearing by the Word of God" (Rom. 10:17).

As a new Christian, I found great inspiration in hearing men of God preach His Word and tell of His faithfulness. My heart was stirred, my convictions deepened, and my faith strengthened as I listened to these servants of Christ.

Three special efforts strengthened my faith when I heard: praying before the preaching, taking notes on the message, and sharing the highlights with someone after the service.

Praying that the Lord will open our hearts to the ministry of the Holy Spirit through the Word will sensitize us to listen and perceive. The Book of Revelation carries Jesus' clear admonition: "'He that hath an ear, let him hear what the Spirit saith unto the churches'" (3:6). The Bible was given by the Spirit of God, and this Author is our indwelling Teacher.

Taking notes helps me to remember more of what is said and to think it through as it applies to my life. A speaker has spent hours in preparation—and years in learning. It seems to me that his efforts are too valuable to entrust to my poor memory. A Chinese proverb says, "Pale ink is stronger than the most retentive mind."

Mature Christians taught me: "Nothing is fully yours until you can give it away." Joe can't give Elmer's Bible to Peter because it doesn't belong to him. And until I have a secure hold on truth—until it is really mine—I cannot pass it on. Sharing a truth I have been taught reinforces my own understanding and possession of it. So—pray, write, and talk about the faith-building Word of God you hear.

2. *We can read the Word regularly and expectantly.* Bible reading can be an inspiration and comfort to us, but I know that for some it is a baffling obligation. We believe it's good for us, but too often it's tepid and flat instead of sparkling and tangy. We need the psalmist's experience: "How sweet are Thy words unto my taste! yea, sweeter than honey to my mouth!" (Ps. 119:103)

Several steps will help make God's Word sweet to you.

• Before reading, pray.

The psalmist is our example for this: "Open Thou mine eyes, that I may behold wondrous things out of Thy law" (119:18). Ask the Lord to give enlightenment and sensitivity. Spiritual truths cannot be comprehended by mere intellect. The Holy Spirit gives discernment that transforms plain statements into personal treasures. The most wonderful result is that we will see Jesus more clearly and love Him more deeply.

Pray for an attentive mind. Luke says of Jesus: "He taught daily in the Temple . . . for all the people were very attentive to hear Him" (Luke 19:47-48). I would like to listen to Jesus the same way that men in the Marine Corps hang on every word of their captain when he gives orders.

Also, pray for a spirit of expectation. David admonished himself: "My soul, wait thou only upon God, for my expectation is from Him" (Ps. 62:5). Knowing the immeasurable wisdom and power of God, David approached Him with an open heart.

When my daughter was young, her eyes would sparkle as Christmastime drew near. She could hardly wait for Christmas Eve and the excitement of opening her gifts. Though the Word of God comes in a "plain wrapping" and we think we know its contents, its discoveries and delights far excel those of the most fabulous Christmas. Our heavenly Father is ready to satisfy our immediate and pressing needs through prayer and His Word.

• Form and follow a purpose for each Bible reading.

Look for something specific. Most people don't find anything special in the Scriptures because they are not looking for anything in particular. For example, reading and reflecting on the way men poured out their souls in the Scriptures will help you to talk with God as with a trusted Friend. The Gospels show us how Jesus witnessed naturally and forthrightly. The life of David, who touched the highs and lows of human experience, teaches careful readers how to become "a man after God's heart," as David was. Ponder the life of Abraham, the "friend of God," to learn how to build an intimate relationship with the Almighty. Seek for something in your reading—and you will find.

• At times, use an organized plan.

I use a reading plan that gives me daily assignments both in the Old and New Testaments. This simple program helps me read through the Bible in a year, so that I have the opportunity to glimpse all of the light God has given for our paths.

We are told, "All Scripture is given by inspiration of God, and is profitable *for doctrine, for reproof, for correction, and for instruction in righteousness,* that the man of God may be perfect, throughly furnished unto all good works" (2 Tim. 3:16).

Doctrine teaches us the truths about God, man, evil, and all the great questions of life.

Reproof warns and rebukes us for wrong and dangerous steps.

Correction directs us back to the narrow and straight path when we have unknowingly stepped off.

Instruction trains and disciplines us in the righteous and joyful life.

The child of God, therefore, neglects God's Word at a serious loss to himself and the handicapping of his service to others.

• Systematically study the Word of God.

Bible study differs from reading. Reading the Bible gives a segmented or a panoramic view of the Scriptures—depending on the amount of area covered—as well as personal guidance and inspiration for living. Bible *study* gives depth of understanding in the Scriptures, acquainting the student with God's great plan, man's great dilemma, and the believer's great heritage in Christ.

Proverbs 2:1-5 points toward this great treasure. "My son, if thou wilt receive My words and hide My commandments with thee, so that thou incline thine ear unto wisdom, and apply thine heart unto understanding; yea, if thou criest after knowledge and liftest up thy voice for understanding; if thou seekest her as silver, and searchest for her as for hid treasures; then shalt thou understand the fear of the Lord, and find the knowledge of God."

Note the action words in verse four: *seek, search, understand, find.*

Seek—as for silver. Search—as for hidden treasure. The person who seeks for hidden riches needs strong motivation, proper tools, and a chart of action.

Through Bible study we can come to a deeper understanding of God, His sovereignty, His purity, and His love for us. We find a solid foundation in these realities for our own lives, so that we remain steady when storms of disappointment and adversity swirl about us.

Proper tools help in Bible study as in any demanding task. Christian publishers have produced many study manuals and helps that give you the benefit of others' cumulative skills.

A series of question-and-answer guides started a study program for me. I went on to chapter-analysis, a topical study, and other methods that stimulated my interest and progress.

A good Bible concordance is almost essential for Bible study in depth. An information-packed Bible handbook or dictionary adds insight and sparkle to Bible investigation. These helps are secondary in value, however, to the direct communication with God in His Word.

We also need charted paths that have proved their effectiveness for other students. One regular path to follow is a specific time during the day set aside for Bible study. My wife studies in the morning after our son leaves for school. My schedule allows study after the evening meal. When I worked in a department store, I took part of my lunch hour for Bible study.

If we do this, we're in good company. Paul commended the Christians at Berea, saying: "These were more noble than those in Thessalonica, in that they received the Word with all readiness of mind, and searched the Scriptures daily, whether those things were so" (Acts 17:11).

• Another path we should take is memorizing the Word of God.

Some beautiful passages in the Bible reveal God's desire for us to plant His words in our hearts. Note Proverbs 7:1-3: "My son, keep My words, and lay up My commandments with thee. Keep My commandments and live, and My law is the apple of thine eye. Bind them upon thy fingers; write them upon the table of thine heart."

God's Word in our heart will be a powerful force upon our lives. Proverbs goes on to promise: "When thou goest, it shall lead thee; when thou sleepest, it shall keep thee; and when thou awakest, it shall talk with thee" (Prov. 6:22).

When the devil tempted our Lord three times, Jesus replied, "It is written . . . " each time. It proved very effective. Dawson Trotman, The Navigators founder, used to say, "When confronted with the devil, don't argue—quote." That's good strategy —for Scripture memorizers!

• Another path we should travel while studying is to meditate on the Word of God. This is important because:

To love and obey God overshadows everything else in life;

The Old and New Testament Scriptures are the divine revelation of God;

We are what we think, and thinking about God and His ways makes us more and more faithful as His people.

Meditating means to digest the Word of God in our mind, turning it over and over to experience its full flavor. God gave this tremendous promise to Joshua. "This Book of the law shall not depart out of thy mouth, but thou shalt meditate therein day and night, that thou mayest observe to do according to all that is written therein; for then thou shalt make thy way prosperous, and then thou shalt have good success" (Josh. 1:8).

The Fellowship of Prayer

The Bible tells us to pray without ceasing. Impossible? God means we should not stop praying because of discouragement or sin or any impediment, and that we can develop an attitude which keeps us in close touch with God.

Prayer truly does change things and people— including the person who prays.

Jesus prayed alone: "And in the morning, rising up a great while before day, He went out, and departed into a solitary place, and there prayed" (Mark 1:35).

He prayed before major decisions: "And it came to pass in those days, that He went out into a mountain to pray, and continued all night in prayer to God, and when it was day, He called unto Him His disciples, and of them He chose 12, whom He also named apostles" (Luke 6:12-13).

Jesus prayed in the midst of a busy schedule: "But so much the more went there a fame abroad of Him, and great multitudes came together to hear, and to be healed by Him of their infirmities, and He withdrew Himself into the wilderness, and prayed" (Luke 5:15-16).

Jesus prayed to His heavenly Father in the midst of important—but secondary—things.

God speaks to us in His Word; we speak to Him in prayer. This two-way communication deepens our fellowship with our Creator, Redeemer, and Friend.

Tools for Fellowship

The Navigators publishes an excellent reading plan designed to guide you through the Bible in either one or two years.

Small group Bible studies which require individual preparation are one of the most effective means of helping a person come to know the Lord or to grow in discipleship. Two study series have been widely used by individuals and groups are: *Studies in Christian Living* and *Teach Yourself the Bible.*

The first is a series of six question-and-answer study booklets plus four study books which teach a simple approach to inductive analysis of Bible chapters. The series builds progressively from one book to the next.

Teach Yourself the Bible is a series by Keith L. Brooks, and is published by Moody Press in Chicago. This excellent series covers both topics and books of the New Testament, using question-and-answer approach primarily.

Appointment with God, also published by The Navigators, introduces Christians to the practice of daily meditation. Four approaches to daily devotions and help in developing one's own plan are very useful.

The Navigators' *Topical Memory System* is said to produce greater dividends for the amount of time invested than any approach to the Bible. Sixty carefully selected verses in six categories cover key areas of the Christian life. Guidance on how to memorize can help one develop his own plan for a lifetime habit of Scripture memorizing.

This thing is needed: fellowship with your Lord. Neglect this and you will always be struggling with your problems instead of celebrating the Lord's victories in you and through you.

11

CHANGING OUR WORLD

The Chinese have a proverb: "When there is peace in the heart, there is peace in the home. When there is peace in the home, there is peace in the neighborhood. When there is peace in the neighborhood, there is peace in the city. When there is peace in the city, there is peace in the land."

That proverb suggests there must be little heart peace these days. There is turmoil and confusion in the world. Our TV sets provide a daily documentary of global strife.

Jesus also said something frightening about man's heart problem: "'From within, out of the heart of men, proceed evil thoughts, adulteries, fornications, murders, thefts, covetousness, wickedness, deceit, lasciviousness, an evil eye, blasphemy, pride, foolishness'" (Mark 7:21-22).

The Bible records that God took a look at man's heart soon after the dawn of human history and saw a bleak picture. "And God saw that the wickedness of man was great in the earth, and that every imagination of the thoughts of his heart was only evil continually" (Gen. 6:5).

The Prophet Jeremiah revealed: "The heart is deceitful above all things, and desperately wicked; who can know it?" (Jer. 17:9)

If a way were found to purify the hearts of humanity, the world could be changed. If a serum could be injected or a potion swallowed that would cleanse humanity of evil and selfishness, the last Nobel Peace Prize could be awarded. There would be no more war, murder, wickedness. A lasting peace would dominate hearts as well as nations.

With this special kind of "heart problem" in mind, note Acts 15:8-9: "And God, which knoweth the hearts, bare them witness, giving them the Holy Ghost, even as He did unto us; and put no difference between us and them, purifying their hearts by faith." Faith in Jesus Christ has power to purify the heart . . . and your witness can bring people to place their faith in Him. What a privilege! And what power!

Paul may have heard a rumor circulating about him: "Oh, he does OK in out-of-the-way places like Thessalonica and Berea, but he doesn't dare go to Rome. In Rome they worship power. The Gospel would be smothered there."

Possibly in answer to such criticism, Paul makes it plain that he is eager to go to Rome. "So, as much as in me is, I am ready to preach the Gospel to you that are at Rome also. For I am not ashamed of the Gospel of Christ: for it is the power of God unto salvation, to everyone that believeth; to the Jew first, and also to the Greek" (Rom. 1:15-16). Paul may have thought, *If they want to see power, wait until they see the effects of the Gospel message. Then they will know what real power is.*

Only one power in the world can make bad men good—the Gospel of Jesus Christ. You and I know that message, and it has been committed to us for carrying to sin-sick individuals. Jesus Christ is the world's only Great Physician, and He freely invites all: "Come unto Me" (Matt. 11:28).

God's Heart Power

From the ministry of Paul at Antioch, his singular mission and message is clear. Speaking about Jesus, Paul said, "Though they found no cause of death in Him, yet desired they Pilate that He should be slain. And when they had fulfilled all that was written of Him, they took Him down from the tree, and laid Him in a sepulchre. But God raised Him from the dead.

"Be it known unto you, therefore, men and brethren, that through this Man is preached unto you the forgiveness of sins; and by Him all that believe are justified from all things, from which ye could not be justified by the law of Moses" (Acts 13:28-30, 38-39).

Paul did not discuss social reform, intellectual fine points, or political matters with people afflicted by sin. He was as concerned about social injustices and political repression as anyone, but he knew that evil individuals produce an evil society and that the Gospel is the only way to change individuals.

Remember what happened when Paul and Silas preached in Philippi? They were beaten and thrown into prison. But God shook the prison with an earthquake, releasing the prisoners. The jailer was converted to Christ when "they spake unto him the Word of the Lord" (Acts 16:32).

That was a demonstration of power! The jailer was the kind of man who could lock two bleeding men in cruel confinement, then sleep like a baby.

The same man, convicted and changed by Christ, washed the prisoners' wounds; he took them into his home for food and fellowship. He experienced a radical change of heart—and his conduct immediately changed.

The world must hear this message today if society is to change. Honorable politicians dedicate their careers to curing the nation's ills. Social reformers labor to alleviate serious problems. But they are working on only the symptoms. The disease defies human control.

Another example of the Gospel's power is found in Ephesians 2. The Jews and Gentiles had nurtured a bitter hatred for centuries. To "God's chosen people," the Gentile was an idol-worshiping dog. A daily prayer of Jewish religious leaders was, "I thank God I am not a Gentile, a slave, or a woman."

After Paul's conversion to Christ, the one-time partisan rabbi declared: "There is neither Jew nor Greek, there is neither bond nor free, there is neither male nor female; for ye are all one in Christ Jesus" (Gal. 3:28).

Paul tells how Jesus obliterated hatred between some Jews and Gentiles. "Wherefore remember, that ye being in time past Gentiles in the flesh, who are called uncircumcision by that which is called the circumcision in the flesh made by hands; that at that time ye were without Christ, being aliens from the commonwealth of Israel, and strangers from the covenants of promise, having no hope, and without God in the world; but now in Christ Jesus ye who sometimes were far off are made nigh by the blood of Christ.

"For He is our peace, who hath made both one, and hath broken down the middle wall of partition between us; having abolished in His flesh the enmity, even the law of commandments contained in ordinances, for to make in Himself of twain one new man, so making peace" (Eph. 2:11-15).

Religious and social hatred dissolved within the new unity in Christ. That's power. God has entrusted that power to us in the Gospel of Christ for a world bleeding from hatred and oppression. Witnesses for Christ can be God's channel for making new people who remake society.

Power Behind the Iron Curtain

A few years ago I visited East Berlin with three friends. We had tea in the Warsaw Coffee House, and our East Berlin guide chatted with us about the Wall, the people in East Berlin, and Communism and its doctrines. I felt a strong urge to witness to our Communist guide, but I was scared, having heard stories of people who had been "detained." I sat there fidgeting, my throat growing dry, but I knew I had to speak for Christ.

During a lull in the conversation, I asked what was the guide's objective in life. He thought a while, and then said it was to do his job well and enjoy a few pleasures such as the theater and recreation—nothing spectacular. He asked what mine was, and I told him I wanted to change the world.

"Change the world!" he exclaimed. "How do you propose to do that?"

I told him that in order to change the world you must change people, because people make up society. One must see a deep moral change brought about in the hearts of men. I said there was only one way to do that, through the Gospel of Jesus Christ. I then told how Christ had changed my life. He listened with great interest, and when

I was finished he asked me what my religion was. When I named my denomination, he said he had never heard of it. I told him that it didn't matter— what counted was that I was a Christian.

He was shocked. "Christian?" he said. "I thought Christians were only concerned with 'pie in the sky by and by.' I didn't know Christians were concerned with what goes on in the world or were trying to do anything about it."

At that point one of my companions, a burly guy, impatiently pounded his umbrella on the floor and exploded, "Pie in the sky! Who do you think it was who said, 'I am come that ye might have life and have it more abundantly'?"

"Who?" asked the startled guide.

"Jesus Christ!" my friend exclaimed.

From there the conversation proceeded to a deep witnessing experience as we Christians all shared the message of Christ. We didn't see a decision, but the Communist accepted a Christian booklet to read.

This man represents thousands of people who think the church has no solution to anything. They don't realize that Jesus said dogmatically, "'I am the Way, the Truth, and the Life'" (John 14:6). They have seen and heard only a distorted version of Christianity. They need to hear and see the real thing in Christian disciples.

God's Solution to Mankind's Disease

All of the social ailments that plague our society— war, racism, crime, drug addiction, poverty, and exploitation—sink their roots deep in rebellion against God. Jesus Christ is the answer—and the only answer—to this universal disease of humanity. When the Son of God lives in man, human rebellion and satanic influence are overcome by superior power.

One young man I talked with at Kansas State University took issue with me. "Mr. Eims, I disagree with your basic premise. It seems to me that you are saying sin is the basic problem in the world and the answer is salvation. I don't believe that. I think that the basic problem is ignorance and the answer is education."

"Well," I told him, "I have no argument against the value of education. But there is one quick way we can put your theory to the test. Let's put on our coats and walk over to the men's dorm and spend some time in the halls listening to the conversations. We'll hear guys talk about the tests they cheated on the other day, or the party they attended last weekend where they got drunk, or how they exploited a woman on their last date. Then you can tell me if education brings about a deep moral change in men. If you're right, the men's dorm at K State should be an apex of morality for the state of Kansas, since everyone here is busily engaged in getting an education."

I picked up my coat.

"Wait a minute," he said.

"What's the problem?" I asked.

"Well, I get your point," he answered.

I explained that a trained mind must not be confused with a transformed nature. I told him of a college professor who said, "I get the idea that all we're doing around here is changing devils into clever devils." The student laughed, and then we began to discuss the life-changing power of the Gospel of Christ. I challenged him with the idea that a real man would want to be part of the solution rather than part of the problem. That night, after a serious conversation, he became a Christian.

A Worldwide Impact

We never know what long-range and broad impact our witness may have. The Apostle Peter ministered to a crippled beggar, and consequently thousands of observers listened to the Gospel and turned to the Lord. "Many of them which heard the Word believed; and the number of the men was about 5,000" (Acts 4:4).

A family in Missouri employed a woman to help with their housecleaning once a week. This Christian's worker's joyful spirit baffled the housewife. She asked the cleaning woman what the secret was to her positive spirit. She answered, "It's the Lord."

The housewife soon learned that her helper enjoyed listening to the "Back to the Bible Broadcast," so on occasion they listened together. When she heard the message of salvation and pondered it, she trusted in Christ.

Through a series of events, the husband came to Christ also and grew rapidly in spiritual strength. Today this couple is ministering for God all over the world. The husband's position in aeronautical engineering has given him opportunities to witness where most Christians have no access. And it started with a faithful Christian hired to clean house. Her reward in heaven will exceed that of some Christian scholars!

I read a story of a father trying to nap on a rainy Sunday afternoon. His little son was constantly disturbing him with the complaint that he had nothing to do. His dad said, "Do anything!"

The boy replied, "There isn't anything."

The dad, noticing a map of the world in the Sunday paper, took it and tore it into pieces. He then challenged his son to put it back together. The little boy sat down and happily began his project while the dad settled down for a long nap.

Shortly the boy piped up: "Dad, it's all finished!" And sure enough, it was.

His dad was amazed as well as irritated. "How did you get it done so quickly?" he groused.

"There was a picture of a man on the back," replied the boy, "and when I got the man right, the world was right too."

Simple, but how difficult in real life! Yet Jesus Christ can make men right. "If any man be in Christ, he is a new creature" (2 Cor. 5:17). "'The things which are impossible with men are possible with God,'" Jesus said (Luke 18:27).

Embracing the World

I remember Dawson Trotman talking an entire evening at a conference about the power of Christian witness. He pointed out that the Lord Jesus told us not only to be witnesses but to make disciples. When we take time with those we lead to Christ to help them grow in Christ, we multiply our witness in startling fashion.

Dawson took quite a bit of time explaining the power of spiritual multiplication. If I were to win a person to Christ, for example, spend six months helping him grow in faith, and then each of us were to win another, there would be four Christians. If we spent six months with the new converts and then the four of us each won another, we would be eight. Continuing on that schedule, we would reach the population of the world in about 16 years!

In practice, of course, the plan breaks down because men do. But the principle is exciting even on a small scale: win one and help him grow and learn to win another.

God wants to multiply your life in other individuals. One of the Scriptures Trotman shared with us was 2 Timothy 2:2: "And the things that thou hast heard of me among many witnesses, the same commit thou to faithful men, who shall be able to teach others also." From Paul, to Timothy, to faithful followers, who in turn add living links in endless witness.

A friend who used to be an instructor at the Air Force Academy asked a group of us a question: "If you were to take a piece of very thin paper, thinner than Bible paper, and fold it 50 times, how thick would it be?" We had no way of knowing, so he told us: the paper would be 17 million miles high! I was impressed again of the tremendous potential of multiplying our witness.

Paul shares this principle as he practiced it: "We preach, warning every man, and teaching every man in all wisdom; that we may present every man perfect in Christ Jesus; whereunto I also labor, striving according to His working, which worketh in me mightily" (Col. 1:28-29).

The apostle here points to the two-fold aspect of Christ's commission:

Warning every man to turn to Christ from his sin and be restored to a personal relationship with God who loves him and yearns for his love;

Teaching converts in the wisdom of God is the second part, to bring God's people to maturity and fruitfulness in Christ. This is the full commission—preaching and teaching—which Jesus gave to His followers. This is the divine plan which will bless the world!

While reading Mark 1:14-15 I was struck by a piercing thought. The passage says: "Now after that John was put in prison, Jesus came into Galilee, preaching the Gospel of the kingdom of God, and saying, 'The time is fulfilled, and the kingdom of God is at hand; repent ye, and believe the Gospel.'"

"Amazing!" I said to myself. "Jesus, who knew everything, could have explained the marvels of the universe to the listeners. He could have given them lectures on Greek philosophy or prophesied the date of Rome's collapse, but He called on them to *repent and believe the Gospel.* That was the one thing they needed for life fulfillment. So Jesus told them.

If we follow this example of Jesus, we may hope to repeat the general sense of His words when we, too, meet the Father: "'I have glorified Thee on earth. I have finished the work which Thou gavest Me to do'" (John 17:4). What a way to go!

12

GROWING TOGETHER

Two young couples hear the Gospel and ask Christ into their lives. A Christian neighbor takes a personal interest in one couple. He and his wife pray for them, invite them to their home for fellowship, and join in Bible study with them. The old-timers answer the questions asked by most new babes in Christ. They introduce them to a good Sunday School class and get them involved in an outreach to others.

No one pays special attention to the other couple in their newfound faith. They stumble, naturally, and no one is near enough to help them. The Bible offers 1700 pages of mysterious phrases to their eyes. At first they go to church on Sunday morning, but after a month or so they occasionally sleep in. Nobody seems to miss them.

After a year we look in on these hypothetical couples—whose prototypes can be found in many churches. One couple is enthusiastic about their new life and is telling others. They can be counted on to respond as people's needs are made known.

The second couple still attends church fairly

regularly. Their prayer experience reaches its high point at the dinner table: "Bless this food, which now we take, to do us good, for Jesus' sake. Amen." The wife recalled it from childhood by sheer will power, and it seems better than awkward phrases seized out of the air. Their new life has stagnated and they are not telling the Gospel to others.

There was not so much difference in the conversions of the couples as in what happened to them after they arrived in the Body of Christ. One couple received loving counsel and friendship, and the other did not.

The spiritual pediatrics given a new Christian to establish him in vital fellowship with the Lord and help him become a faithful witness is usually called "follow-up." It might also be called survival training, because spiritual growth, health, and reproductivity depend on it.

Four Follow-up Methods

The Bible gives a great deal of guidance in the matter of follow-up. There are four methods taught in the New Testament.

One method is personal contact. Paul wrote, "For I long to see you, that I may impart unto you some spiritual gift, to the end ye may be established" (Rom. 1:11).

Paul's second and third missionary journeys were follow-up visits to groups of young Christians for whom he felt a personal responsibility. At the beginning of his second journey he said to Barnabas, "Let us go again and visit our brethren in every city where we have preached the Word of the Lord, and see how they do" (Acts 15:36).

Just as a doctor visits his patients to speed their progress or prevent a relapse, Paul was diligent to get around to see these people. If he found them wandering, he would help them get back on the right track. If he found them wavering, he would bolster their faith. If he found them winning, he would cheer them on.

Another method of follow-up is letter writing. Luke was concerned about a friend named Theophilus. He wrote a letter to him and gave as a reason: "That thou mightest know the certainty of those things, wherein thou hast been instructed" (Luke 1:4). That letter to Theophilus is the Gospel according to Luke. Later Luke wrote to him again, and his letter is the Acts of the Apostles. Luke must have had quite a burden for this man's spiritual development to take the time to write such detailed and lengthy letters.

Much of our New Testament consists of the Apostle Paul's follow-up writing to young Christians.

A third method of follow-up is sending another person. Quite often we lead a person to Christ, and because of distance we are unable to see him again. Possibly we know someone who can go and help him.

Paul sent Timothy to the Thessalonians when he couldn't go. "Wherefore when we could no longer forbear, we thought it good to be left at Athens alone; and sent Timotheus, our brother, and minister of God, and our fellowlaborer in the Gospel of Christ, to establish you, and to comfort you concerning your faith" (1 Thes. 3:1-2).

The fourth way to follow-up a person is through prayer. This is undoubtedly the most important. Paul speaks often in his letters about his regular praying. For example, he wrote, "We give thanks to God always for you all, making mention of you in our prayers; remembering without ceasing your work of faith, and labor of love, and patience of hope in our Lord Jesus Christ, in the sight of God and our Father" (1 Thes. 1:2-3).

On occasion he would tell them what he was asking God. "For this cause we also, since the day we heard it, do not cease to pray for you, and to desire that ye might be filled with the knowledge of His will in all wisdom and spiritual understanding; that ye might walk worthy of the Lord unto all pleasing, being fruitful in every good work, and increasing in the knowledge of God; strengthened with all might, according to His glorious power, unto all patience and longsuffering with joyfulness" (Col. 1:9-11).

To the Ephesians, Paul revealed this impassioned prayer concern: "For this cause I bow my knees unto the Father of our Lord Jesus Christ, of whom the whole family in heaven and earth is named, that He would grant you, according to the riches of His glory, to be strengthened with might by His Spirit in the inner man; that Christ may dwell in your hearts by faith; that ye, being rooted and grounded in love, may be able to comprehend with all saints what is the breadth, and length, and depth, and height, and to know the love of Christ, which passeth knowledge, that ye might be filled with all the fullness of God" (Eph. 3:14-19).

Two words, "exhort" and "confirm," give insight into the follow-up work of the New Testament Church. "Exhort" means to urge and encourage; "confirm" means to strengthen and make secure. They describe the ministry of Paul and Barnabas in many cities. "They returned . . . confirming the souls of the disciples, and exhorting them to continue in the faith, and that we must through much tribulation enter into the kingdom of God" (Acts 14:21-22).

Paul's third missionary journey was largely devoted to follow-up, as indicated in Acts 18:23. "And after he had spent some time there, he departed, and went over all the country of Galatia and Phrygia in order, strengthening all the disciples." Paul knew that the new Christians would have difficulty growing in a pagan environment and facing persecution. Converts today also need personal help—just as any newborn infant.

Using God's Word in Follow-up

John wrote about some young Christians whose spiritual strength had won notable victories over the devil. "I have written unto you, young men, because ye are strong, and the Word of God abideth in you, and ye have overcome the wicked one" (1 John 2:14). The same wily enemy sets traps for new Christians today, and the way to victory is the same: "The Word of God abideth in you."

To "abide" is to live and thrive, and only follow-up training will establish God's Word in the heart of a new believer during the wobbly walk of his first days.

Paul acknowledged the power of God's Word in the Thessalonian Church. He said: "For this cause also thank we God without ceasing, because, when ye received the Word of God which ye heard of us, ye received it not as the word of men, but as it is in truth, the Word of God, which effectually worketh also in you that believe" (1 Thes. 2:13). We can expect God's Word to pour spiritual power into a believer like a great dynamo of energy, fueled by God Himself. In the physical absence of Paul, the written Word of God exhorted and confirmed the young converts, generating warmth in their souls and shedding light on their daily paths.

An excellent means of communicating God's Word is through group Bible study. There are three general types of Bible studies, and I pray you will specialize in the third one.

1. *The Mama Bird Study.* The young converts gather regularly with the experienced Bible teacher, who shares an important truth that nourishes and strengthens them . . . much as the mother bird flies into the nest and drops a worm into an open beak of her young. This study is helpful but does not teach the new babe how to study the Bible for himself and learn to feed his own soul. The new Christian may become totally—and harmfully—dependent on the teacher.

If a person is thirsty, I can bring him a glass of water or help him find a water source. If I do the former, I will soon have to bring another glass. If I do the second, he will soon have his own supply.

The new convert needs both to be fed and to learn to feed himself.

2. *The Share-Your-Ignorance Study.* Here the group gathers, and the leader asks, "What chapter are we going to discuss this week?"

One person says, "I think it's chapter four."

Another says, "No, I think it's chapter three."

"No, we did that last week, didn't we? Isn't that where Jesus talked to Nicodemus about being born again?"

"You're right. It is chapter four."

Once that is settled, the leader says, "Has anyone read it?" Since no one has, he says, "OK, let's read it together, and then we'll discuss it." They do that, and proceed to share their lack of knowledge with each other.

3. *The Share-the-Blessing Study.* The leader gives assignments for the group to prepare before the members meet. After prayer, members share the fruit of their preparation with each other. Each member is enriched by the comments of the other members. They learn to study the Bible for themselves, both alone and in the group. The applications are practical, and the participants encourage each other in their growth in the family.

Scripture memorizing is a solid-meat diet for getting the Word of God into the lives of new Christians. I thank God for every passage the Lord has enabled me to write on the table of my heart.

Some prisoners of war from Vietnam said, "Bible verses on paper aren't one iota as useful as Scriptures burned into your mind where you can draw on them for guidance and comfort."

I have watched new Christians, fortified by memorized Scripture, witness to their friends. They would say very naturally, "Yes, I used to think the same thing until I found out the Bible says . . ." and they would quote a pertinent passage of Scripture. And the authoritative Word of God witnessed as only it can.

The Word of God in the memory also helps a convert in his battle against sin. Though he has become a partaker of Christ's divine nature, his old nature is still present and active. He is tempted by his old habits and by new ruses of the enemy. Victory or defeat will be shaped by the kind of nourishment he has been receiving.

Food for the old, sinful nature is on every hand. Magazines, books, motion pictures, billboards, television, jokes among friends, and many other things can feed our old nature. There is one main food for the new nature: the Word of God. Spiritual en-

couragement and counsel from Christians strengthen
our spirit, but that, too, issues from the Word of
God. Fresh food direct from the Father's hand is
tastiest.

Fellowship in Follow-up

A young Christian needs the fellowship of the local
church. I have not seen a person do well over the
long haul trying to go it alone. We are a spiritual
body, and we are dependent on each other. Getting
established in a good church is a must for the new
convert.

Through sermons he can be taught the Word of
God and receive enlightenment and exhortation
from the pastor. He can be made aware of the
worldwide outreach of the Gospel and learn the joy
of giving money to the Lord to advance His world
mission.

New friends' lives will challenge him to stead-
fastness, and can reveal to him how Christians live.
As he matures, he has an outlet for the talents and
gifts God has given him for serving and building
up the body of Christ. All of these work together to
make a healthy member of the living Church.

Communion with God in Follow-up

A consistent quiet time with God will build a
friendship with our Maker-Redeemer. Converts
need frequent encouragement and guidance to establish this daily pattern as it is one of the most
difficult of Christian practices to maintain. But it
is one of the most rewarding.

When my daughter was in high school, we
planned a routine that helped me be consistent in
my quiet time and also gave time to fellowship in
the Word with her. She rode an early bus, so I

would join her for an early breakfast. I'd have a cup of coffee and read my New Testament portion for the day to her while she ate. We would discuss it and also have a brief prayer together before she ran out the door. After she left, I would go to the front room and continue my time with the Lord.

Bible study, Scripture memorizing, joining a Bible-preaching church, and quiet time all help to get the new convert established, but they shouldn't be emphasized at the same time. It's wise to find something the convert "takes to" at first and major on that for awhile before introducing a second program. Babies can be made sick by force feeding— spiritual as well as physical. Trying to cram in too much at once can discourage a new Christian. Some "parental" or older brother discernment will suit the pace of training to the individual student-disciple. In the process, your enthusiasm for these things will stir an appetite for them in his heart.

Help from an Older Christian

Often a group Bible study or the church services do not meet the deep personal needs of a new Christian. He needs individual attention, like a doctor's patient. A doctor does not go to the waiting room and give general health rules to his roomful of patients; he counsels them one by one and prescribes appropriate remedies for each. Again we're reminded of Paul's example:

"Ye know how we exhorted and comforted and charged every one of you, as a father doth his children, that ye would walk worthy of God, who hath called you unto His kingdom and glory" (1 Thes. 2:11-12).

Lorne Sanny, president of The Navigators, had an experience in California that illustrates this need for individual help. A youth leader invited Sanny to work for a week in his high school Bible club work. When Lorne arrived, he discovered he was booked morning, noon, and night with meetings. Lorne asked if something could be worked out so he would have some time with individual kids, and the leader juggled the schedule.

One of the students that Lorne met with was a girl who was showing great promise.

When the two sat down to talk, Lorne asked, "How's it going?"

"Not so good," the girl replied.

"What's the matter?"

The girl told him about a boyfriend who was going to junior college and seeing her on weekends. She was trying to help him spiritually, but frequently the two got involved with each other physically, and that was bothering the girl deeply.

This girl was attending two Sunday services, the young people's meeting, and midweek prayer meeting in her church, plus two Bible clubs a week. But the positive effects of six meetings a week were being undermined by increasing sensuality in her life.

This girl knew she needed help, and she poured out her heart to this counselor she could trust. Lorne shared Scriptures with her about Christ's claim on our bodies and gave specific help on the threat of carnal pleasure to spiritual vitality.

Young Christians often need such individual attention to help them meet new problems.

Some Christians recognize witnessing as their responsibility but fail to see the great need for follow-up ministry. They may say: "They are the Lord's children, so I just commend them to Him for His care."

Paul's life and words show the fallacy of such reasoning. "Therefore watch, and remember that by the space of three years I ceased not to warn every one night and day with tears" (Acts 20:31).

Christ's great apostle goes on to say: "And *now*, brethren, I commend you to God, and to the Word of His grace, which is able to build you up, and to give you an inheritance among all them which are sanctified." Only after *three years* of sharing his life and knowledge with these new Christians, did Paul commend them to God and to the Word of His grace—and move on to witness and train elsewhere.

Like Paul, we must help young Christians get established in the fellowship of the local church and in daily fellowship with the Lord through His Word and prayer. And, like Paul, we must be experiencing the realities that we encourage in others.

The man who got me started in Scripture memorizing introduced me to it by saying, "Here's something that has proven to be a great help in my life." I was interested, and I found the same rich blessings through his example and guidance.

I once asked a Christian what the greatest joy of his life was, and he said it was winning souls for Christ. I agreed that this was a great blessing, but I said I had experienced an even greater blessing: "Seeing those I have led to Christ go on in their walk with the Lord and win others."

He had never thought of this, and was challenged by it. Later we got together and went over some of the principles of follow-up. Today there are Christians all around the world who have been led to Christ by men he has trained in follow-up.

Have you ever been in the obstetrics ward of a hospital when a baby was born? The whole place mobilizes to protect the young life. Nurses wear face masks to restrict germs; disinfectant pervades the atmosphere; special formulas are available for feeding; there's a special room for the new baby. Everything is organized to get the new-born babe off to a strong start.

That's follow-up. And that's Jesus' way to win men and women, boys and girls, in your own "Jerusalem, Judea, and Samaria" and to the farthest corner of the earth. Perhaps *our generation* will complete this task and see the return of our Lord! Maranatha!

New follow-up books suitable for reading or elective study are *Born to Grow* by Larry Richards ($1.75) and *Disciples are Made—Not Born* by Walter Henrichsen ($1.75). Both published by Victor Books. Available at Christian bookstores, or order from Victor Books, P.O. Box 1825, Wheaton, Ill. 60187. Add 15¢ postage for each book.